"I love shellfish! The very word is sheer poetry. They are fished and caught by skilled professionals, they are lovingly and carefully cooked, and they are relished by gourmets and gourmands. Shellfish are food for the gods and, to us humans, a foretaste of heavenly bliss."

Mannerström's SHELLFISH

Recipes Leif Mannerström

Food and still-life photography Tomas Yeh

Settings photographer Lisa Nestorson

Stylist Sarah Bergh

Text Jesper Lindberg

English translation Roger Tanner

FIREFLY BOOKS

Shrimp, Sophia Loren and craftsmanship

My first big shellfish experience occurred when I was 9 or 10 years old. I blew a week's worth of allowance on shrimp and sat down with them on some steps in the Helsingborg docks. I ate them with reverence, sucking the last drop of goodness out of each and every one of them. And in those days two-and-a-half crowns would buy you a fair number!

At 15 I had my first introduction to making real lobster soup. The cook split the lobsters while they were still living, which I thought was rather grisly. "Shouldn't you boil it first?" I asked. "No," came the reply, "you can't boil a pig before you butcher it!"

We used the green coral of the female lobsters for a soup made with butter and cognac. When the soup boils, its color changes from green to red. That was a thrilling sight — shellfish are marvelous to work with! My job was to pour on the cognac and Madeira after the cook had sampled them — well, that's the way things were in those days.

One of the first places I worked at was the Maritime restaurant in the Strand Hotel in Nybroviken, Stockholm; in its day it was the finest shellfish restaurant of all. I was put in charge of the shellfish counter, which I made up every day — a wonderfully enjoyable task for a boy. My passion for shellfish was compounded one day when I was told to arrange a shellfish platter for Sophia Loren, who was staying at the hotel. She was the dream woman at that time!

I put so much love and hard labor into that platter that when the chef saw it he told me to go in and serve it myself. She was so delighted, she held the dish aloft, creating a golden photo opportunity; the dining room was lit up by the popping flashbulbs. The pictures were published everywhere, and a tremendous fuss was made when people noticed that Sophia Loren hadn't shaved her armpits.

I already knew at a tender age that this was my vocation, and I was only 23 when I became chef at the Henriksberg restaurant, where I was the youngest person in the kitchen. Restaurant kitchens were a tough proposition in those days: eat or be eaten — it was that kind of hierarchy!

Sjömagasinet is the biggest fish and shellfish restaurant in Sweden. Given that we serve fresh shellfish, offerings are very much dependent on wind and weather. It is a point of honor to let a customer know that a certain raw material may not be obtainable on a certain day.

People often moan about shellfish prices, but anyone who has been out in a fishing boat, pulling up lobster pots in the rain and gale-force winds only to harvest perhaps four lobsters in 30 pots, will know what heavy work it is. Who would be prepared to work for that kind of money? No, that sort of fishing is a craft that deserves our full respect! There's an old joke that says there was once a fisherman from Fjällbacka, near Göteborg, who went out fishing in really stormy weather. Turning to his friend, he said, "You know Larry, I wouldn't want to be ashore in dirty weather like this." Ha!

I have innumerable memories and could go on telling stories indefinitely, but this book isn't really about me. Instead the leading characters of the play between the covers are the shrimp,

Actors Ulf Palme and Alf Kjellin look on as a radiant Sophia Loren brandishes the basket of shellfish that Leif Mannerström has just brought to her table. A happy evening in the 50s at the Maritime restaurant in Stockholm.

the lobsters, the crayfish, the Norway lobsters, the mussels, the oysters and the crabs! My own tales and anecdotes from a long life at the stove will one day be collected in my memoirs, at present code-named *A Scullion Remembers.*

Remember that no recipe is sacred; you do not have to follow it implicitly. You can, in which case it will turn out as if I had made it. But a recipe can also be thought of as inspiration, or why not as hands-on poetry? You have to be inquisitive when cooking, ready to experiment. Crayfish are a raw material offering numerous possibilities. And just think of all the exciting things to be created with shellfish that can be bought live.

Or else you can just boil them and eat them with lemon. Or maybe an aïoli …

Or perhaps, as the old saying goes, the tastiest results are achieved by doing as little as possible with the very best ingredients.

Göteborg, August 2008
Leif Mannerström

Introducing the cast of this play between the covers

Lobster

Swedish lobster is good, but its being the best is a myth. Lobsters caught in Sweden, Ireland, Denmark, Norway, Scotland and Brittany — all European lobsters, in fact — are one and the same breed.

The American lobster, on the other hand, is something quite different. The reason why lobsters grow to such an enormous size in Maine is the suitability and warmth of the water, and, additionally, this is a faster-growing species.

My wife Lilian and I shared an 11-pound (5 kg) lobster at The Palm in Maine, and it was excellent.

But just as Norrland berries get tastier from growing more slowly in a somewhat colder climate, so the lobsters growing more slowly in our cooler waters develop more flavor.

As for deep-frozen imported lobster, I wouldn't touch it with a 10-foot pole.

"Lobster and crayfish are both nourishing and sustaining, though not to such a degree as has been imagined; they contain a balsamic fatty oil which renders them somewhat indigestible and, to some people, choleric, for which reason they should be ingested with due circumspection."
— Dr. Ch. Em. Hagdahl, *Kok-konsten som vetenskap och konst,* 1891

Crayfish

Linnaeus disapproved of crayfish, proclaiming that, "Man shall not eat insects." Poor him — just think what he missed. But Carl Michael Bellman knew better:

That little croft without the gate,
Where scarlet crayfish on the stove await …

When people on the west coast of Sweden talk about or advertise "crayfish," one should remember that what they really mean is Norway lobster. Freshwater crayfish aren't all that highly thought of on the west coast. But a little farther inland, where the lakes glitter and the streams babble, setting out crayfish pots is one of the principal delights of August.

If you buy frozen crayfish, give them two days to thaw out in the fridge, so as to bring out their proper flavor.

"The anatomy of the crayfish has been a subject of many an aficionado's conjecture. For the time being it would appear proven that the crayfish has been given two claws as justification for two substantial helpings of Swedish schnapps."
— *Dagens Nyheter*

"In folklore, crayfish have always been credited with manifold remarkable powers. Using these so-called crayfish stones, necromancy could be practiced, diseased cattle restored to health and ailing poultry reinvigorated.

"An old academic lecturer divided natural bodies into: (1) simple bodies, such as mountains, (2) composite bodies, such as dogs and cats, and (3) peculiar bodies, such as windmills and crayfish."
— *Hagdahl*

Shrimp

Cooking shrimp is a fine art from the word go, hinging on how the fisher boils them in the boat and what salt he or she uses.

I use only fresh shrimp, as fresh as I can get them. You can use frozen ones when I'm looking the other way, but only when making quick dishes one day midweek, perhaps a rainy Tuesday that needs a bit of gilding. Just remember, though, if possible, let the shrimp thaw slowly. That gives them the fullest flavor.

But as I said, use fresh shrimp whenever possible. And remember that this is a delicacy to be indulged in not more than, say, three times a week.

And — don't throw the shells away: they're a wonderful ingredient for making soup or stock with.

"Shrimp also occur off the west coast and belong to the crustaceans, but are appreciably smaller than our ordinary crayfish. They are used in the same way as the latter for soups and sauces, and are also a popular dish for the breakfast or tea table."
— *Hagdahl*

("Breakfast" [Sw. *frukost*] in Hagdahl's day meant "lunch.")

8

Oysters

Oysters are graded according to size: 0 means really big ones, and these are best employed as ingredients for various dishes, while 1 is a bit smaller and 2 is, in my opinion, the appropriate size for eating *au naturel*. If, as Hagdahl claims, one can get through 144 oysters without feeling full afterwards, it must be the smallest grade he is referring to.

"Of oysters. There are few other foodstuffs at one and the same time so easily digestible and so nourishing. They stimulate the appetite and the water in them promotes digestion. It is typical of this foodstuff that the advent of repletion is so delayed that a practiced oyster eater can easily consume 144 (12 dozen) and then readily set to with the proper repast, as though nothing had been ingested."

— Hagdahl

Interest in oysters is growing, and oyster-opening competitions have become a sporting event in their own right. Skill, speed and strength are combined with the gourmet's delight. (And the gourmand's too, if there are several dozen to be savored!)

Oysters are a delight, as well as being beneficial, low on calories and highly nourishing. For the oyster-eating novice, they can be served grilled with Danish remoulade sauce; see page 248.

Norway lobsters

Perhaps the most wonderful raw material the west coast of Sweden can offer. A source of great happiness and enjoyment. A shellfish with immense possibilities — au naturel, au gratin … Just keep turning these pages and you'll find a good many recipes. In short, this is a great favorite of mine.

If instead of cooking your Norway lobsters yourself you buy them ready-cooked, remember that their tails should be curled; they must be rigid and unyielding. Test them. If they "give" or feel loose and floppy, go for something else.

Norway lobsters are caught from the coast of Norway down to Öresund (the strait between Sweden and Denmark).

Mussels

Mussels at their best are nearly my favorite shellfish. The possibilities and variations are infinite. And they're not hard to come by. Blue mussels (also known as common mussels) are sold in net bags nearly everywhere, or at least in specialty fish stores.

Razor clams, included in this book, are more of a rarity, but have a wonderful shellfish flavor. Try them if you happen to see them at the counter.

I learned to love scallops when working with the Swedish America Line. They were especially popular with Americans. We took fresh ones on board at every port of call, and we got through every amount of them.

The scallops on sale here in Sweden come mostly from America, but scallops also swim in Swedish waters, and they are caught in large quantities in Norway, though the Norwegian ones are very expensive.

Crab

Crab — what a marvelous word! It has the fragrance of September, of wonderful dinners when the leaves are turning, the wind gets up and one is glad to be sitting indoors. Light the candles, get out the duly chilled white wine, mix a shellfish sauce and eat your crab as it is, whole or divided. Or cook something with it!

Nowadays one can also simplify matters by shopping for just crab claws. So long as you have a nutcracker handy!

When shopping for your crab, bear in mind that it must not have been frozen. If it has, go for something else. Put some pressure on at your specialty fish store: it will no doubt be prepared to order fresh crab if you ask for it if it operates on the principle of giving the customers what they want.

Ask the employees at the fish store to test the crab's "fatness" or "heaviness"; perhaps you can ease the shell and look for yourself. The crab shouldn't slosh about when shaken.

And as usual, it goes without saying that you want female crabs with their delicious roe!

Table of Contents
(catagorized by main ingredient)

A few splashes of freshly squeezed lemon juice — what could be simpler? Sometimes the bright, pure and tart tang of lemon is all you need to top off fresh, just-cooked shellfish.

Think of it as a ladder of tastes. You start with just a lemon, which is as quick and easy as it gets.

The next rung on the ladder is a pure mayonnaise, homemade of course. This is easier than you think; see the recipe on page 245. And then you can go on scaling the culinary heights with the various sauces, flavorings and accompaniments that are offered in this book.

But remember, sometimes one lemon is all you need.

Joppe's shrimp salad serves 4

Tore Wretman created this salad in 1947 at Teatergrillen, in honor of the newly appointed Director of the Stockholm Dramatic Theatre (Dramaten), Ragnar "Joppe" Josephson. It was served very often after that and always unmixed!

The Restaurateur by Royal Appointment would only use newly peeled, fresh shrimp.

Of course!

Ingredients:
2.2 lb (1 kg) absolutely fresh shrimp in their shells
12 large button mushrooms, finely minced
6 finely-grated radishes
½ cucumber, finely minced
4 finely-minced and de-seeded tomatoes
½ c (115 g) runner beans, lightly cooked and minced
½ c (120 mL) Dijon vinaigrette (see page 246)
2 tbsp (30 mL) salmon roe

Garnish:
1 bunch of dill

Serve with:
Rhode Island sauce (see page 248)
toast

Procedure:
Peel the shrimp.
Arrange the shrimp and vegetables nicely on a serving dish.
Drizzle with the vinaigrette.
Garnish with roe and dill sprigs.
Serve (preferably) with Rhode Island sauce to one side and with toast.

Mussel crêpes serves 4

When I started in the kitchen, every self-respecting restaurant had crêpes on its menu. This recipe is a memento from the Maritime restaurant, the leading fish and shellfish restaurant in its day.

   Crêpes with mussels were the most popular version, along with Prince Bertil's crêpes (with shrimp).

Crêpes ingredients:
3 eggs
2 tbsp (30 mL) white flour
⅔ c (160 mL) whipping cream
⅓ c (80 mL) milk
1 pinch of salt
1 pinch of superfine sugar
1 tbsp (15 mL) soda water
butter and oil for frying

Mussel filling ingredients:
2.2 lb (1 kg) raw blue mussels, cleaned
   and removed from their shells
2 tbsp (30 mL) butter
4 shallots, finely chopped
5 cloves of garlic, minced
½ bottle white wine
1¼ c (300 mL) béchamel sauce (see page 247)
1 bunch of dill, finely chopped
1¼ c (287 g) grated parmesan cheese
3½ tbsp (50 mL) clarified butter
salt and pepper

Procedure:
Wash the mussels carefully in running water.
Open them by tapping them carefully on the edge of the sink.
Discard any mussels which do not "clam up."
Stir-fry the mussels in 2 tbsp (30 mL) butter with the shallot and garlic.
Pour on the white wine, cover and boil for about 2–3 minutes or until the mussels are cooked and have opened. Add salt and pepper.
Beat the eggs and meal into a smooth batter.
Add the cream, milk, salt and sugar. Pour in the soda water.
Heat for about 3 minutes, until the batter sets into fine crêpes.
Stew the mussels in béchamel sauce.
Add the dill and season to taste.
Put the filling into the crêpes and transfer to a serving dish.
Sprinkle with the cheese and drizzle with the clarified butter.
Bake in the middle of the oven at 425°F (220°C) until the cheese turns golden.

Hint:
Save the gorgeous mussel stock for a soup or sauce.

Shellfish cake serves 4

This is an exclusive "meat cake" (*pannbiff*) of scallops,
Norway lobsters, oysters, lobster and crab. We prepared
this dish for a party which included the King of Sweden.
He is a good cook himself and really appreciated this
number, so it was duly renamed "the King's Delight."

You mix the chopped shellfish with mustard and egg,
to hold the "meat cake" together.

It's a good idea to drain the chopped shellfish in a
colander. Dried panko breadcrumbs will give the cakes an
extra crispness.

Ingredients:
8 large oysters
2 pre-cooked lobsters (see page 249)
6 pre-cooked Norway lobsters (see page 249)
6 scallops
1 fat crab, boiled
4 egg yolks
1 tbsp (15 mL) Dijon mustard
1 bunch of chives, finely chopped
1 c (200 g) of dried panko breadcrumbs
1 tbsp (15 mL) butter for frying
salt and pepper

Serve with:
mayonnaise flavored with sweet chili sauce
and lots of watercress

Procedure:
Open the oysters and cut away the beard.
Clean all the shellfish and remove the meat.
Cut up into large pieces. Mix with egg yolks,
mustard and chives in a mixing bowl.
Season to taste.
Shape into four cakes.
Dredge with the panko breadcrumbs.
Fry in butter until it is crisp.
Serve with watercress mayonnaise and sweet
chili sauce, as illustrated.
This makes a wonderful starter or late-night snack.

Scallops Provençale   serves 4

On our first visit to France, in the 70s, this was the first thing Crister Svantesson and I had to eat at the bistro in the same building as our hotel.

Catching the wonderful fragrance of it from our balcony, we went straight down and ordered one each, plus a bottle of Muscadet. After the meal we had an espresso each, smoked a Gauloise and sat there feeling that this was the life. French and uncomplicated! Quite unforgettable.

Blue mussels can be fried the same way, if you like. They turn out scrumptious too!

Ingredients:
20 large scallops
½ c (115 g) button mushrooms, finely chopped
2 shallots, finely chopped
10 cloves of garlic, crushed
⅔ c (160 mL) olive oil
1 bunch of parsley, roughly chopped
2 spring onions, finely chopped
1 tbsp (14 g) white bread crumbs
salt and pepper

Serve with:
baguettes

Procedure:
Fry the scallops, button mushrooms, shallots and garlic in oil for about 2 minutes at a high temperature in a wide-bottomed pan, until they change color.
Add the parsley, spring onion and breadcrumbs.
Season to taste.
Serve with chunks of crisp baguette.

Boiled lobster

It is a good idea to boil your lobster one day in advance, leaving it to soak in its juices overnight. Boiling lobster is an art. The thing is not to boil it for too long, or else it becomes tough.

Boiled lobster is one of the great pleasures of life, preferably a fat female with butter and roe!

Ingredients:
2 live lobsters, weighing about 1 lb (500 g) each
3.17 quarts (3 L) of water
1 bunch of dill, crown dill if possible
½ tbsp (7.5 mL) dill seeds
⅓ c (80 mL) coarse salt

Serve with:
Rhode Island sauce (see page 248)
toast
matured cheese

Procedure:
Bring the water to a boil before adding the dill, dill seeds and salt.
Boil for a few more minutes before putting in the lobsters (first removing any rubber bands from the claws).
Boil slowly over low heat for 5–6 minutes.
Put aside and leave to cool in the stock.
Store in the fridge overnight.
Serve with Rhode Island sauce and toast, matured cheese and a chilled white wine or beer.

Lobster au gratin serves 4

The classic of classics! The number one dish for New Year's Eve. And perhaps the best-loved of all shellfish dishes.

For this recipe, I think one should indulge in fresh lobster, though the imported kind will do at a pinch, or you can even use langouste (spiny or rock lobster), as we often did in Spain.

The lobster must be pre-cooked only, because it will also be heated au gratin, and if overcooked it is likely to be tough.

Ingredients:
2 lobsters, about 1 lb (500 g) each (preferably pre-cooked)
    (see page 249)
1 tbsp (15 mL) butter
½ c (150 g) small button mushrooms, diced
1 onion, finely chopped
1 tbsp (15 mL) white flour
1¼ c (300 mL) whipping cream, whip ⅓ c (80 mL)
    and put aside
3½ tbsp (50 mL) reduced shellfish stock (see page 244)
1 tbsp (15 mL) brandy
1 tsp (5 mL) Madeira
1 tsp (5 mL) pale Dijon mustard
1 pinch of cayenne pepper
1 bunch of dill, finely chopped
salt and pepper

Serve with:
rice or freshly-baked bread

Procedure:
Split the lobsters with a strong, sharp knife, remove
the meat and cut it up into large pieces.
Heat the butter in a pan, put in the mushrooms and
onion and lightly fry.
Add the flour and pour in the cream and shellfish stock.
Add brandy, Madeira, mustard and cayenne pepper
to taste.
Season to taste.
Fold the lobster meat and dill into the mixture, then
add the whipped cream.
Arrange the lobster shells on a large, oven-proof serving
dish and fill them with the mixture.
Bake in the oven at 480°F (250°C), using the broiler
only, if possible, until the color is right.
Serve with rice or warm freshly-baked bread.

Grilled scallops with
lemon-braised fennel serves 4

By now it can't have escaped you that I'm a great scallop
devotee. I have been ever since my early days with the
Swedish America Line, when scallops were served daily
to great rejoicing.

This recipe also has an Asian taste, and grilling brings
out the fresh flavor of the mussels very nicely.

Ingredients:
12 large scallops
2 fresh bulbs of fennel
2 tbsp (30 mL) butter
½ tbsp (7.5 mL) superfine sugar
2 lemons
1 tbsp (15 mL) oil for frying
salt and pepper

Garnish:
2 tsp (10 mL) soy sauce
2 tbsp (30 mL) olive oil
a few strips of coriander leaf
1 chili, minced

Procedure:
Shred the fennel as thinly as possible and lightly fry
in the butter.
Season with care.
Add the sugar and simmer for a while.
Cut the lemon peel into thin slices (best done with a
zest grater) and squeeze out the juice.
Flavor the fennel with just the right amount of acid
from the lemon juice.
Season the scallops.
Brush the grill pan with oil and grill the scallops in
the hot pan for about 15 seconds on each side.
Arrange the scallops with the fennel.
Mix the soy sauce and oil together and drizzle over
the scallops.
Garnish with lemon peel, coriander leaves and chili.

Norway lobster and scallops in a lemon vinaigrette serves 4

Mexican ceviche is a variation on this theme.
Store in the fridge for an hour or two — this allows
the lemon flavor to ripen. The shellfish are not raw after
this treatment; they mature after marinating. Brilliant!

   Then afterwards put your feet on the table, bring on
the castanets and pass the tequila!

Ingredients:
8 raw scallops, cut up into large pieces
8 raw Norway lobsters, peeled and cut up into large pieces
1 tbsp (15 mL) lime juice
½ tsp (2.5 mL) grated lime peel
1 tbsp (15 mL) orange juice
2 tbsp (30 mL) olive oil
1 crushed garlic clove
2 yellow tomatoes, diced
2 red tomatoes, diced
1 celery stalk, thinly sliced
2 limes, peeled and de-cored
1 chili, finely chopped
a few bunches of fresh coriander
salt and black pepper

Garnish:
4 cocktail tomatoes, scalded and peeled (optional)

Procedure:
Mix the lime juice, lime peel, orange juice, olive oil
and garlic together in a mixing bowl.
Add the scallops, Norway lobster tails, vegetables,
chili and coriander.
Season to taste.
Put in glasses and chill for about 2 hours before serving.
Garnish with tomatoes (optional).

Crab and Norway lobster salad

serves 4

Crab is fattest and tastiest in autumn. That makes autumn a good time for this substantial salad, which is made even better when accompanied by Norway lobsters.

This makes a wonderful starter, with two of our loveliest shellfish clasping claws.

Ingredients:
2 fat crabs, females if possible
4–8 Norway lobsters, freshly boiled and peeled
½ c (150 g) young spinach leaves, rinsed
½ c (150 g) coarsely chopped raw sugar snap peas
salt and pepper

Sauce:
¾ c (180 mL) homemade mayonnaise (see page 245)
½ c (120 mL) low-fat crème fraîche
1 tbsp (15 mL) sweet chili sauce
1 tsp (5 mL) good curry powder

Serve with:
crusty freshly-baked bread
butter or olive oil

Procedure:
Extract the meat from the crab and claws.
Cut up into large pieces.
Remove the meat from the Norway lobsters and cut up.
Mix the ingredients for the sauce.
Fold in the shellfish meat and season to taste.
Arrange as illustrated, with the spinach, sugar snap peas and Norway lobster tails.
Serve with crusty freshly-baked bread and good butter or olive oil.

Mussels and french fries
serves 4

This recipe is my version of the Belgian national dish on offer at Brussels' fast-food restaurants. The combination of french fries and mussels is a bit odd, but I love eating mussels straight out of their shells with crunchy french fries and sharp sauce.

If you have visitors, the fragrance of the mussels cooking in the kitchen leaves everyone feeling happy and relaxed. And do make your own french fries — they'll be much better than the store-bought ones!

Ingredients:
4.4 lb (2 kg) blue mussels, thoroughly cleaned
2 shallots, finely chopped
3 cloves of garlic, crushed
3½ tbsp (50 mL) olive oil
½ chili, thinly sliced
⅓ c (80 mL) dry white wine
salt and pepper
1 bunch of parsley, roughly chopped

Garnish:
1 c (230 g) crispy bread croutons

Serve with:
french fries
sharp sauce (see page 249)

Procedure:
Wash the mussels carefully in running water.
Tap them carefully on the edge of the sink to open them.
Discard the mussels that do not close.
Fry the shallot and garlic in the olive oil.
Add the mussels and chili and pour on the wine.
Cover and cook for 2–3 minutes or until the mussels are done and have opened.
Add salt and pepper.
Serve warm in a big bowl, pour over the parsley and croutons, and serve with crisp, homemade french fries, sharp sauce and a nice cold beer.

Panko-fried Norway lobsters
with mango salsa serves 4

Panko is a type of breadcrumb from Japanese cuisine
that you can buy in Asian shops and other well-stocked
supermarkets. It makes deep-fried food a lot crunchier
and tastier.

   Anything deep-fried must be eaten as soon as possible
after it is ready and served while still hot!

Ingredients:
12 pre-cooked Norway lobster tails (see page 249)
¼ c (60 mL) white flour
2 beaten eggs
1 c (200 g) panko breadcrumbs
oil for deep frying

Salsa:
1 ripe mango
1 chili
1 clove of garlic, crushed and minced
1 bunch of coriander, minced
½ c (120 mL) sweet chili sauce
2 tbsp (30 mL) olive oil
salt and pepper

Serve with:
deep-fried strips of leek
wedges of lime

Procedure:
Make the salsa first:
Cut away the peel from the mango.
Cut the flesh into little pieces.
De-core the chili and chop it finely.
Mix the salsa ingredients together.
Dredge the Norway lobster tails in the flour,
the beaten egg and the panko, in that order.
Now deep-fry in hot oil for about 2 minutes.
Serve the Norway lobsters with the salsa and
(optional but desirable) with deep-fried strips
of leek and lime.

Spanish garlic shrimp serves 4

One of the best-known, best-liked and most highly-appreciated dishes in my Gran Canaria restaurant. I must have served several tons of shrimp this way. It works best if you can get hold of raw shrimp, but of course you can use boiled ones.

 This dish has to be served instantly, while it's still piping hot.

Ingredients:
1¾ lb (800 g) raw scampi or raw shrimp
1⅔ c (400 mL) good olive oil
20 coarsely chopped cloves of garlic
1 roughly-cut chili
coarse salt
black pepper
2 bunches of roughly-cut parsley

Serve with:
lemon or lime
freshly-baked bread

Procedure:
Heat the oil in a big frying pan.
Put the garlic and chili in first.
Fry them until they are transparent but
without letting them change color.
Add salt and a few twists of the peppermill.
Sprinkle generously with parsley and serve
with lemon or lime and warm freshly-baked bread.

Sashimi of Norway lobsters serves 4

For this recipe the Norway lobsters have to be very lightly cooked — just pre-cooked. The idea is for them to be nearly raw to do full justice to the purity of their own innate flavor.

 This dish is a wonderful composition where Japan meets Sweden!

Ingredients:
12 large Norway lobsters, pre-cooked (see page 249)
⅓ c (100 mL) olive oil
2 tbsp (30 mL) soy sauce
1 chili, finely chopped
2 tbsp (30 mL) roasted sesame seeds
1 clove of garlic, crushed and chopped
1 tbsp (15 mL) grated horseradish
1 piece of fresh ginger, about ½ c (115 g), grated
1 bunch of chives, roughly cut
salt and pepper (optional)

Serve with:
warm garlic bread

Procedure:
Split the Norway lobsters.
Gut them and arrange the halves on a serving dish or plate.
Mix the olive oil, soy sauce, chili, sesame seeds, garlic, horse-radish and ginger together.
Season to taste (optional).
Pour the mixture over the Norway lobsters and sprinkle with the chives.
If you like, serve with warm garlic bread and a good white wine or beer.

Norway lobster tails fried in butter and served with grated horseradish

serves 4

This dish, featuring both browned butter and horseradish, offers a classic contrast of flavors.

Horseradish is a traditional herb which has long been used in Swedish kitchens, and the possibilities and permutations are numberless.

And this time, with fried fresh Norway lobster tails — all I can say is that simple, more often than not, is best.

Ingredients:
16 large raw Norway lobsters, split and with
    innards removed
½ c (115 g) butter
2 tbsp (30 mL) freshly-grated horseradish
salt and pepper

Garnish:
lettuce
sprigs of dill
vinaigrette (see page 246)

Procedure:
Brown the butter in a wide-bottomed frying pan.
Fry the Norway lobsters until golden brown.
Add salt and pepper.
Arrange on a serving dish, pour the butter over
the lobsters and sprinkle with the horseradish.
Garnish with a little lettuce, dill and the vinaigrette.

Razor clams with grapefruit salad
serves 4

Razor clams aren't all that common. If they are hard to come by, use another kind of mussel. Ordinary blue mussels, of course, will do just as well.

Surprise your guests and let a thousand flavors blossom. Who said flower power was dead?

Ingredients:
20 fresh razor clams
⅓ c (80 mL) dry white wine
2 grapefruits, blood grapefruits if possible
½ c (120 mL) olive oil
1 tbsp (15 mL) good balsamic vinegar
1 crushed clove of garlic
salt and pepper

Garnish:
1 chili, de-cored and thinly sliced
2 thinly-sliced spring onions
a few edible flowers for garnish (consider using
    violet or nasturtium)

Procedure:
Cook the mussels in the wine for about 10 minutes.
Clean and rinse the mussels well, cut the flesh
into big pieces.
Peel the grapefruit and cut up into neat segments.
Mix a little grapefruit juice, the olive oil, the
balsamic vinegar and garlic together.
Season to taste.
Arrange on a serving plate as illustrated, pour on
the dressing and garnish with chili, spring onion
and flowers.

Omelette with curried crab serves 4

Behold, an omelette with a slightly more elegant touch!
You can put the omelette pan straight on the table to
allow everyone to experience the alluring fragrance of
curry from the crab mixture.

This makes a good starter, a light lunch or a buffet
attraction. Or eat it just for its own sake, at the end of a
hard day, with a nicely chilled beer.

Ingredients:
1 boiled crab (with the meat removed and cleaned)
6 eggs
1 tbsp (15 mL) water
1 tbsp (15 mL) butter for frying

Curry mixture:
1 tbsp (15 mL) butter
1 tsp (5 mL) curry powder
2 tsp (10 mL) flour
¾ c (180 mL) whipping cream
2 tbsp (30 mL) shellfish stock, bought
    ready-made, or else see page 244
salt and pepper

Garnish:
watercress

Procedure:
Melt the butter in a saucepan.
Add the curry powder and quickly fry.
Stir in the flour and pour on the cream
and reduced shellfish stock.
Stir for a couple of minutes while it thickens.
Season to taste.
Fold in the crab meat.
Break the eggs and pour on the water.
Whisk the egg batter lightly. Add salt and pepper.
Fry the omelette in the butter, preferably in
a non-stick pan.
Pour on the curry mixture and garnish with watercress.
Serve straight from the pan.

Sesame-fried scallops with ginger and spring onion serves 4

My wife Lilian and I adore Asian food, and this recipe has an Asian touch. We are often in London, and this recipe recalls a successful restaurant meal we had there. Try it, but — and this is very important — don't over-fry the mussels.

Serve with a chilled pale beer.

Ingredients:
12 large scallops
1 bunch of spring onion, cut into coarse rings
½ c (120 mL) olive oil
1 crushed clove of garlic
2 tbsp (30 mL) sesame seeds (lightly roasted if possible)
1 tbsp (15 mL) butter
¾ c (180 mL) soy sauce
1 piece of fresh ginger, peeled and finely grated
salt and pepper

Procedure:
Fry the spring onion in a little of the oil.
Add the garlic, salt and pepper.
Turn the mussels in the sesame seeds.
Fry them in butter in the frying pan over medium heat for about half a minute on each side, or until they turn golden brown.
Mix a dressing of soy sauce, olive oil and ginger.
Drizzle it around the scallops.

Cockles à l'Español
in a lemon vinaigrette serves 4

Anyone who has been to Spain is bound to have come across this tasty shellfish, prepared here in the simplest way possible. Just be sure to soak them properly, so as to get rid of the sand.

Ingredients:
4.4 lb (2 kg) cockles
3.17 quarts (3 L) cold water
½ c (120 mL) 12% proof distilled vinegar
1 onion, minced
4 crushed cloves of garlic
⅓ c (80 mL) olive oil
¾ c (180 mL) white wine
juice of 2 lemons
2–3 celery stalks, cut into rings
2 chopped tomatoes
1 bunch of parsley, roughly chopped
salt and pepper

55

Procedure:
Mix the water and vinegar in a mixing bowl.
Put in the cockles and leave them to stand for an hour or so. Any sand they contain should seep out.
Rinse the cockles well in a colander with cold water.
Drain thoroughly.
Fry the onion and garlic in oil without letting them change color.
Add the cockles, wine, lemon juice, celery and tomatoes.
Add salt and pepper.
Cover and simmer for 2–3 minutes, until the cockles have opened.
Sprinkle with parsley.
Serve with the bread.

Shrimp-trawling is hard work.

Every Monday the *Rio* sets out from Smögen, and the three-man crew has a number of arduous days ahead of it. They trawl for between 7 and 10 hours, at which point the trawl is wound in and the catch is dealt with. The shrimp are graded according to size. Sea urchins, Norway lobsters and other species are kept separate.

The shrimp are cooked in brine for about 10 minutes at a time. Then they are rinsed in cold water to cool them quickly, and put straight into cold storage.

And so it goes for a number of days until the quota is reached, at which time the boat sets course for Smögen again.

A proper shrimp sandwich serves 4

Everyone loves a shrimp sandwich. There should be a
society for the Friends of the Shrimp Sandwich. I for one
would join it immediately! But my word, the perversions
of the name that are dished up every day throughout the
length and breadth of Sweden!

   A shrimp sandwich must be made with good white
bread. And only with mayonnaise and Rhode Island sauce
— no butter on the bread.

   A proper shrimp sandwich is food for the gods, a
foretaste of heaven for us ordinary mortals!

Ingredients:
2.2 lb (1 kg) absolutely fresh shrimp in their shells
¼ c (60 mL) homemade mayonnaise (see page 245)
4 slices of preferred bread
4 lemon wedges
4 sliced radishes
8 fresh green asparagus stalks, lightly boiled and sliced
8–12 lettuce leaves
sprigs of dill

Serve with:
Rhode Island sauce (optional) (see page 248)

Procedure:
Peel the shrimp.
Spread the mayonnaise on the bread (no butter!).
Put on plenty of peeled shrimp, as illustrated.
Garnish with lemon wedges, radishes, asparagus,
lettuce and dill.
Serve with the Rhode Island sauce, if any.

Shrimp soup serves 4

This recipe will teach you how to make a reduced stock with shrimp shells. (Never throw them away, or I'll report you!) This is a relatively simple recipe.

I've said it before and I'll say it again: this soup always turns out well. Remember to serve it piping hot. A well-made shellfish soup always goes down well, and your "stock" will rise accordingly.

Ingredients:
1⅓ lb (600 g) fresh shrimp
2 tbsp (30 mL) olive oil
1 onion, finely chopped
1 piece of fresh fennel, finely diced (about 3½ tbsp or 50 g)
1 tsp (5 mL) tomato purée
2½ c (600 mL) fish stock (you may use stock cubes
    if you like)
½ c (120 mL) dry white wine
1¼ c (300 mL) whipping cream
a little brandy (optional)
salt and fresh-ground pepper to taste

Garnish:
1 bunch of dill, minced

Procedure:
Peel the shrimp, saving the shells.
Store the shrimp in a cool place for the time being.
Fry the shells in oil in a saucepan for a minute or so.
Add onion, fennel and tomato purée.
Fry for a couple more minutes.
Add the fish stock and wine, simmer everything
for 10 to 12 minutes.
Strain.
Return the stock to a saucepan.
Pour in the cream and cook for about 10 minutes.
Season to taste, perhaps also adding a dash of brandy.
Arrange the shrimp nicely and garnish with dill.

Scallops Rossini serves 4

Duck liver and truffle is a classic combination, but here's another version. After all, a scallop is pretty much the same shape as a tournedos.

Two gentle flavors meet together on crispy toast, and with truffle sauce added …

Ingredients:
4 scallops
4 pieces of duck liver, 2 oz (60 g) each
2 slices of toast, crusts removed
½ c (120 mL) red wine sauce (see page 248)
1 tsp (5 mL) truffle oil
sea salt and pepper

Garnish:
fresh thyme

Procedure:
Sear the duck liver quickly, on both sides, over high heat in a dry pan together with sea salt and pepper, until it is a nice color.
Now fry the scallops and bread in the fat from the duck liver.
Let it turn a nice color.
Add salt and pepper.
Heat the red wine sauce and flavor with truffle oil.
Put the duck liver and scallops on the bread.
Drizzle the sauce around the dish.
Garnish with thyme.

Shellfish lasagna   serves 4

There's a bit of preparation involved in making this lasagna, but once it's in the oven you can focus your attention on your guests. And when it's done, it's done!

This is a wonderful dish for dinner parties.

Ingredients:
12 lasagna sheets, fresh if possible
⅔ c (150 g) fresh spinach, coarsely chopped
1¼ c (287 g) grated leek
juice of ½ lemon
1 eggplant, sliced thinly
1 tomato, sliced thinly
salt and pepper

Tomato and shellfish sauce:
14 oz (400 g) shellfish — e.g. mussels, shrimp
    and Norway lobsters — boiled and coarsely
    chopped
1 onion, coarsely chopped
2 pressed cloves of garlic
olive oil for frying
2 cans of crushed tomatoes, drained
½ c (120 mL) heavily reduced shellfish stock
    (see page 244)
⅓ c (80 mL) dry white wine
1 tbsp (14 g) chopped fresh basil
1 tbsp (14 g) plucked thyme leaves
2 tbsp (30 mL) Demerara sugar

Béchamel sauce:
3 tbsp (45 mL) butter
2 tbsp (30 mL) white flour
1 tsp (5 mL) fennel seeds
2½ c (600 mL) creamy milk [1¼ c (300 mL)
    whipping cream and 1¼ c (300 mL) milk]
1 bay leaf
2 whole sprigs of dill
¾ c (180 mL) grated parmesan cheese
salt and pepper

Procedure:
Start with the tomato and shellfish sauce:
Fry the onion and garlic in a saucepan until translucent.
Add the other ingredients except the shellfish.
Simmer gently for about 15 minutes.
Add the chopped shellfish and season to taste.
Put the sauce to one side.
Now the béchamel sauce:
Fry the butter in a saucepan, stir in the flour and fennel seeds.
Dilute with the creamy milk and whisk to a smooth sauce, eliminating any lumps.
Add the rest of the ingredients, except for the parmesan cheese which is mixed in last, and simmer for about 10 minutes, stirring continuously.
Add the parmesan cheese and bring to a boil.
Season to taste and strain.
Put aside.
Fry the spinach and leek in olive oil.
When the leaves begin to soften, add the lemon juice and season to taste.
Set the oven to 400°F (200°C).
Grease an oven-proof dish, about 7.9 x 11.8 inches (20 x 30 cm) in diameter.
Arrange the béchamel sauce, shellfish sauce and spinach mixture in between the sheets of lasagna.
Start with a thin layer of béchamel and finish with a thick one.
Before putting the lasagna in the oven, you can garnish, as illustrated, with a few slices of eggplant, zucchini and tomato.
Sprinkle all over with a little grated parmesan.
Bake in the middle of the oven for about 30 minutes until the surface bubbles and has turned a nice color.
Serve in the dish or on plates with a little lettuce.

Garnish:
a little extra shellfish
perhaps a little parmesan from the cheese slicer

Serve with:
lettuce

Scrambled egg, flavored with chives and served with shrimp roe fills 4 eggs

Take care to save the shrimp roe — the finest delicacy imaginable, and a great delicacy with a strong flavor.
If you're serving shrimp anyway, this is the perfect starter.

Ingredients:
4 eggs
¾ c (180 mL) whipping cream
1 bunch of chives, finely chopped
salt and pepper

Garnish:
1 slice of kavring rye bread
eggshells
2 tbsp (30 mL) shrimp roe
8 peeled shrimp
1 sprig of dill
chives

Procedure:
Set the oven to 215°F (100°C).
Cut the bread into thin sticks and put them on a baking sheet.
Dry them in the oven for 10 or 15 minutes.
Break the eggs into a mixing bowl.
Put the bowl into a saucepan containing a little water (a water bath). Whisk over low heat until it starts to thicken and turns creamy.
Add the cream, a little at a time, whisking continuously.
Keep whisking until the mixture thickens, then add the chives and season to taste.
Put the scrambled egg into the empty eggshells from which a bit of the shell has been removed.
Garnish with the shrimp roe, shrimp, sprig of dill and chives.
Poke the sticks of bread down into the mixture.

The empty shells of 2.2 lb (1 kg) shrimp. Don't throw them away — they'll make a wonderful stock.

Shellfish terrine serves about 10

This is easier than it looks! A good terrine looks fancy but isn't hard to make, though you do need a food processor or mixer.

When making terrines, let your imagination run riot. The sky's the limit!

Ingredients:
2.2 lb (1 kg) cleaned scallops without their shells
about 40 peeled raw shrimp (boiled is also acceptable)
10 large raw Norway lobster tails, peeled
about 10 thin slices of lard or air-dried ham
2 c (500 mL) whipping cream
1 tbsp (15 mL) gelatine powder
1 bunch of chives, finely chopped
salt and pepper

Serve with:
herb crème-fraîche or bleak roe sauce
lettuce

Procedure:
Set the oven to 200°F (95°C).
Line a greased oblong terrine mold, holding
about 2.1 quarts (2 L), with slices of lard.
Run half the scallops in a food processor until
finely chopped. The scallops must be fridge-cold.
Add the cream, at fridge temperature, a little at
a time, plus the gelatine powder, salt and pepper
and combine into a smooth mixture.
Stir in the chives.
Slice the remaining scallops.
Fill the mold with alternate layers of mixture
and shellfish.
Insert an oven thermometer.
Cover with a lid or foil.
Bake the terrine in a water bath in the middle
of the oven until the core temperature is 145°F (62°C).
Allow it to cool.
Store in the fridge overnight with a weight on top.
Serve in slices with a cold sauce (perhaps herb
crème fraîche?), bleak roe sauce and crisp lettuce.

Lobster soup serves 4

This is the most elegant of all shellfish soups — the king of all soups.

I learned this recipe at the start of my career and it has accompanied me to all of my different restaurants — Maritime, Strand Hôtel in Stockholm and, of course, Sjömagasinet.

This has remained one of the most popular starters over the years, and we make huge amounts of it.

Note: Try to be generous with the brandy!

Ingredients:
2 small pre-cooked lobsters (see page 249)

For the soup:
4¼ c (1 L) of lobster shell stock (see page 249)
1⅔ c (400 mL) whipping cream
1 tbsp (15 mL) butter
3 tbsp (45 mL) brandy
1 tbsp (15 mL) Madeira
1 tsp (5 mL) cornstarch flour, mixed with 2 tsp
    (10 mL) water
salt and pepper

Garnish:
a few shavings of truffle
cress (optional)

Procedure:
Clean and shell the lobsters.
Cut the meat into neat slices or pieces and put aside.
Cook the lobster stock.
Reduce the lobster stock until about 3⅓ c
(800 mL) remains.
Add the cream and reduce slowly for 5 minutes.
Stir in butter and pour on the brandy and Madeira.
Stir in the cornstarch flour and season to taste.
Heat the lobster meat and transfer to warm bowls.
Pour on the hot soup and the truffle shavings.
Garnish with truffle and cress (optional).

Toast with lightly smoked mussels and marinated mango salad serves 4

If you don't have a simple smoker already, get one. It'll do wonders for your repertoire.

The tangy flavor of the mango goes very well with shellfish, and chili and mango are a great team.

This is a really delicious recipe!

Ingredients:
4.4 lb (2 kg) fresh blue mussels
1 chopped onion
1 tbsp (15 mL) oil

Mango salad:
4 slices of white bread
1 tbsp (15 mL) butter
1 ripe mango, cut in pieces
1 scallion, cut up in rings
1½ chilies, finely grated
½ red (Spanish) onion, cut up
1 tsp (5 mL) sesame oil
salt and pepper
3½ tbsp (50 mL) Dijon vinaigrette (see page 246)

Procedure:
Wash and scrape the mussels clean in running water.
Gently tap the mussels open against the edge of the sink.
Discard any that don't close up again.
Fry the onion in oil in a large saucepan.
Add the mussels, cover and cook gently until steam forms and the mussels open.
Drain off the liquid (which is worth saving for a soup or sauce).
Clean and pluck the mussels carefully.
Smoke them lightly in a smoker.
Mix all the ingredients for the mango salad together with the Dijon vinaigrette.
Season to taste.
Fry the bread until it is crisp in a frying pan.
Arrange as illustrated.

Poached Norway lobsters
with dill mayonnaise serves 4

My grandmother ran a restaurant called Cecilia's Dining
Room in Långholmsgatan, in the Södermalm district of
Stockholm, and this is one of her recipes. It's a wonderful
spring dish to serve when the sun is peeping through. The
lemon, the dill, the wonderful herbs … Serve it cold, and
preferably somewhat jellied. Devilishly good!

Ingredients:
12 large raw Norway lobster tails, peeled
¾ c (180 mL) mayonnaise, preferably homemade
   (see page 245)
1 bunch of dill, finely chopped

Poaching liquid:
1 quart (1 L) of water
⅓ c (80 mL) 12% proof distilled vinegar
3½ tbsp (50 mL) salt
1 small carrot, sliced
1 onion, peeled and sliced
1 lemon, sliced
10 cloves
10 allspice corns
10 white peppercorns
4 bay leaves
1 tbsp (15 mL) dill seeds

Serve with:
toasted crispbread
well-matured cheese

Procedure:
Clean and peel the Norway lobsters, removing
every trace of shell and innards.
Bring all of the liquid poaching ingredients to a
boil in a broad-bottomed saucepan.
Leave to stand for about 10 minutes.
Put the Norway lobsters into the liquid.
Bring to a boil and simmer for about 1 minute.
Remove the saucepan from the heat and let the
Norway lobsters cool in the liquid.
Mix the mayonnaise and finely-chopped dill together.
Season to taste.
Serve with toasted crispbread and well-matured
cheese (recommended).

Toasted rye bread with tomato
and dill-marinated mussels serves 4

Mussels at their best are perhaps my favorite shellfish.
The variations are endless.

A vinaigrette goes well on this toast, while the mussels
rest on a bed of tomatoes. It's a light sauce; a fine dressing.
And on freshly-baked, moist and slightly acidic rye bread,
the combination with the mussels is well nigh perfect!

Ingredients:
about 20 blue mussels, boiled,
    cleaned and shelled
2 tbsp (30 mL) cooking oil
¼ c (60 mL) white wine vinegar
3 tbsp (45 mL) ketchup
3 tbsp (45 mL) chili sauce
2 onions, finely chopped
1 bunch of dill, finely chopped
butter for frying
16 tomatoes, marinated and sun-dried
salt and pepper

Garnish:
dill
tomato chips (tomato peel dusted
    with cornstarch flour and deep-fried in oil)

Procedure:
Mix the oil, vinegar, ketchup and chili sauce with
half the onion and half the dill.
Add the flesh of the mussels to the mixture
and season to taste.
Leave aside to marinate.
Fry the rye bread on both sides in butter in a frying pan.
Put the bread on plates and place sun-dried tomatoes
on top of it.
Top off with the marinated mussels, followed by
the rest of the chopped onion and dill.
Garnish with dill seeds and tomato chips.

Shellfish casserole serves 4

This was a real crowd-pleaser that we served quite often at the historic Johanna restaurant which Crister Svantesson and I ran together for 10 years.

It's tricky to make, but well worth the trouble.

Ingredients:
4 Norway lobster tails, peeled and boiled
15–20 fresh shrimp, peeled
4 oysters, opened and removed from their shells
1⅔ c (400 mL) shellfish stock (see page 244)
4 sheets of gelatine

Garnish:
arugula
light bread, thin slices
carrots
celeriac
chives
cold-pressed canola oil
salt and pepper

Procedure:
Soak the sheets of gelatine in cold water for about 5 minutes.
Bring the stock to a boil and stir in the gelatine.
Put layers of shellfish into ramekins that can hold about ½ c (120 mL).
Carefully pour on the stock.
Store in the fridge for 3–4 hours until the stock has set or better still, overnight.
Turn out the casserole onto plates and serve with a few lettuce leaves and newly fried croutons (the croutons are made from thinly sliced bread which has been dried in the oven for about 15 or 20 minutes).
Finely chop the carrots, celeriac and chives, and dredge them in a little cold-pressed canola oil.
Season to taste.

A hint:
You can simplify matters by lining the ramekins with cling wrap.

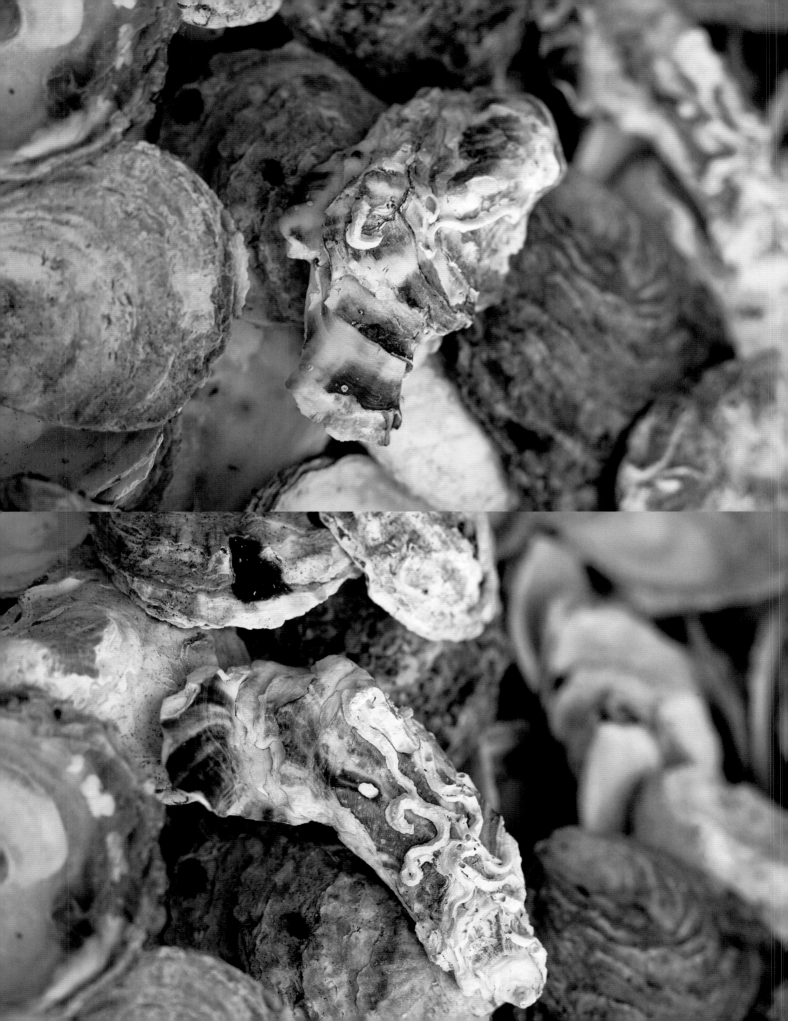

Oysters au naturel
with a shallot dressing

When opening oysters, be sure to have a sharp knife and, preferably, a protective glove. Alternatively, you can fold a tea towel.

When you have "cracked the lock" of the oyster (cut the hinge), be sure to wipe the knife before continuing.

Ingredients:
6 oysters per person

Ingredients for the shallot dressing:
⅔ c (160 mL) water
2 shallots, finely chopped
3½ tbsp (50 mL) good red wine vinegar
1 tsp (5 mL) pale Dijon mustard
a few turns of the black peppermill

Procedure:
Mix the dressing ingredients thoroughly.
Add salt to taste (optional).
Serve with the oysters.

Oysters with salmon roe serves 4

The salty tang of the oysters makes this dish extremely
tasty. Nowadays, with sturgeon roe (Russian caviar)
unobtainable — and the Iranian so dreadfully expensive
— salmon roe fits the bill excellently.

While on this subject, Swedes should be very grateful
and proud of their bleak roe, especially when it's from
Kalix — we don't really need to look any further.

A frothy beer goes well with this recipe!

Ingredients:
12 oysters, neatly opened

Garnish:
¾ c (180 mL) salmon roe
1 red (Spanish) onion, finely chopped
¾ c (180 mL) sour cream
½ c (115 g) small, newly-fried, warm bread croutons
small sprigs of dill

Procedure:
Part the oysters.
Clean them and remove the beard.
Arrange the shells neatly on a dish.
Garnish with the salmon roe, red onion,
sour cream, croutons and sprigs of dill.

Grilled oysters
with Danish remoulade serves 4

Grilling oysters is a good idea, especially for those making their first tentative explorations into the world of shellfish.

The grilled surface gives a special salty tang, and together with the curry in the sauce, the recipe adds up to a fantastic taste experience.

Ingredients:
16 large, round, beautiful oysters
1 c (240 mL) remoulade sauce (see page 248)
½ c (120 mL) sweet chili sauce
2 bunches of parsley, deep fried
2 spring onions, finely grated
1 tbsp (15 mL) cooking oil
salt and pepper

Procedure:
Pluck the parsley leaves from the stalks.
Immerse the parsley in hot oil; it's ready when it's nice and crisp.
Arrange the sauces, parsley and spring onions.
Open the oysters and dry them well.
Grill them lightly on both sides in a pan.
Eat them as soon as they're warm.

Large seared gambas with mojo sauce and Spanish salt potatoes serves 4

I spent two years running a restaurant in Spain, in Gran Canaria, and this recipe reminds me of what that scene often looked like: this dish was served at lunchtime while the sun was blazing and a cold, dry white wine was in the ice bucket. It's an easy recipe, and wonderful summer eating.

Serve with potatoes boiled in salt together with garlic sauce (mojo sauce). But don't go on a date for a couple of days afterwards …

Ingredients:
16 large gambas
1 tbsp (15 mL) coarse salt
2 tbsp (30 mL) olive oil

Serve with:
green or red mojo sauce (see pages 247–248)
Spanish salt potatoes (see page 246)
2 lemons, halved

Procedure:
Heat a broad-bottomed frying pan.
Sprinkle in salt and add a little olive oil.
Sear the gambas for about 1 minute on each side.

95

Warm boiled lobster with a horseradish butter sauce serves 4

Crister Svantesson and I were in charge of the food at Hammersmith Farm in connection with the 1997 America's Cup. We often served this dish to the crews, by request. There was fantastic lobster to be had at roughly the price of carrots …

Ingredients:
2 large freshly-boiled lobsters weighing 1.3 lb
    (600 g) each (see page 25)
2 c (480 mL) beurre blanc sauce (see page 247)
¼ c (60 mL) horseradish, finely grated

Serve with :
crusty, freshly-baked bread

Procedure:
Remove the lobsters while warm and split them
with a strong, sharp knife.
Remove the gut.
Crack the claws.
Arrange on dishes and pour on plenty of warm sauce.
Sprinkle with horseradish. Enjoy!

Shellfish paella serves 8

Another Spanish recipe. The inspiration for this
Spanish shellfish creation comes from the years I
spent running a restaurant on Gran Canaria. This is
my version of "shellfish hash."

This is a wonderful thing to put out for a dinner
party with a few good sauces for company.

Ingredients:
2 lobsters, pre-cooked (see page 249)
    and cut up into large pieces
2.2 lb (1 kg) blue mussels
1–1.3 lb (500–600 g) cockles
16 gambas
2.2 lb (1 kg) clams
6 crushed cloves of garlic
1 small bunch of celery, chopped into large pieces
⅓ c (80 mL) olive oil
¾ c (180 mL) dry white wine
1 bunch of scallions, chopped into large pieces
a few sprigs of thyme
1 c (230 g) cherry tomatoes, halved
salt and pepper

Serve with:
aïoli (see page 245)
crusty, freshly-baked bread

Procedure:
Wash and clean the mussels in cold running water.
Discard those which do not close when you tap
them gently on the edge of the sink.
Soak the cockles in cold water to get rid of any
remaining sand.
Fry the garlic and celery in the olive oil using
a wide-bottomed frying pan or a pot.
Put in all the shellfish and pour on the wine.
Add the scallions and thyme.
Add salt and pepper.
Cover and bring to a boil for about 2 minutes.
Put in the tomatoes and stir.
Serve with aïoli and crusty, freshly-baked bread.

Whelk salad serves 4

Whelks are a bit unusual and often hard to come by. It is important to clean them thoroughly. And if you can't get whelks, make this delightful starter with ordinary mussels — that would also taste delicious.

Alternatively, this dish can be used as a dressing for a bigger salad.

Ingredients:
12 whelks
3 avocados
1¼ c (287 g) mixed lettuce shoots
3½ tbsp (50 g) roasted pine nuts
parsley and chives

Dressing:
juice of 1 lemon
zest of ½ lemon
¼ c (60 mL) cold-pressed canola oil
1 shallot, peeled and finely chopped
2 cloves of garlic, peeled and minced
3½ tbsp (50 g) chopped parsley
salt and pepper

Procedure:
Clean the whelks carefully in cold water.
Boil them for about 2 minutes in generously salted water, and chill them in cold water immediately afterwards.
Mix all the dressing ingredients together in a bowl, season to taste.
When the whelks have cooled, pry them out with a fork.
Cut away the hard disc and looser parts farthest inside the shell.
Slice them thinly and put them in the dressing.
Cut the avocados in half and remove the pits.
Scoop out thin slices from the avocado halves with a spoon and add them to the dressing.
Season to taste.
Arrange the salad attractively with the whelk shells, lettuce shoots, a little parsley and chives.
Sprinkle with roasted pine nuts.

Baked clams
with a hazelnut dressing serves 4

Another recipe from my Spanish period. You have to
remember that as a country, Spain consumes a lot of
shellfish! In Madrid, Galicia or Barcelona, the fish stores
and supermarket counters are teeming and groaning with
shellfish. An inspiration in itself!

Almonds and nuts are popular in Spain, so a hazelnut
dressing is a fairly natural choice.

Ingredients:
4.4 lb (2 kg) large clams, lightly cooked
coarse salt
½ c (115 g) hazelnut kernels, roasted and roughly chopped
1¼ c (300 mL) green mojo sauce (see page 247)

Serve with:
wedges of lime or lemon
warm bread

Procedure:
Set the oven to 440°F (225°C).
Bring the clams to a boil in a covered saucepan
until they open up.
Transfer the clams to a large oven-proof dish on
a bed of coarse salt.
Mix the nuts into the mojo sauce and cover
the clams with this dressing.
Bake in the middle of the oven for about 8 or 10 minutes.
Serve with lime or lemon and warm bread.

Bouillabaisse serves 4

Such a poetic word, bouillabaisse, and what wonderful associations are called to mind by the very mention of this marvelous dish, of which there are so many different versions.

Originally, of course, bouillabaisse was an everyday soup, made by the fishermen's wives with whatever hadn't been sold during the day. The taste is fantastic, and nowadays this is anything but an everyday dish: it's party fare!

We make a very French version at Sjömagasinet, and have actually been told that we make it better than the French themselves. Whether that's true or not, everything stands or falls — as always! — by the quality of the raw materials.

Ingredients for the soup:
2.2 lb (1 kg) fish bones, cleaned and rinsed (scraps of
    sole, turbot and brill, for example, will do nicely)
2.2 lb (1 kg) Norway lobster and lobster scraps
1 fennel bulb, coarsely chopped
1 onion, peeled and coarsely chopped
2 red paprikas, coarsely chopped
1 large carrot, peeled and coarsely chopped
¼ small celeriac, peeled and coarsely chopped
6 cloves of garlic, peeled and crushed
olive oil for frying
½ c (120 mL) tomato purée
3 tbsp (45 mL) paprika powder
2 tbsp (30 mL) mixed fennel seeds
1 tbsp (15 mL) mixed star anise
½ tbsp (7.5 mL) cumin
½ tbsp (7.5 mL) chili powder
½ tsp (2 g) saffron
3½ tbsp (50 mL) concentrated orange juice
2 chicken stock cubes
⅓ c (80 mL) pastis liqueur

Procedure:
Set the oven to 390 °F (200°C).
Spread out the fish and shellfish scraps on three baking sheets.
Roast them in relays in the middle of the oven for about 20 minutes, until the shells have begun to pale and the bones develop a little color.
Meanwhile, stir-fry all the chopped vegetables for about 2 minutes in olive oil in a wide-bottomed saucepan.
Add the tomato purée and all the herbs and spices (except the saffron, which will be put in a bit later) and stir-fry for a few more minutes.
Put in the roasted fish and shellfish bones and add enough water to cover them.
Simmer, covered, for 1 hour.
Strain through a wide-meshed strainer or a colander.
Return the strained liquid to the saucepan and put it back on the heat.
Add the remaining ingredients and reduce the liquid until about 1 quart (1 L) remains.
Run the warm liquid (not too much at a time) in a mixer or blender. Mind you don't burn yourself! You can hold the lid firmly in place with the aid of a folded tea towel to keep the liquid from splashing over the edge.
Combine into a smooth mixture and then return to a saucepan through a fine-meshed strainer.
Add a little olive oil, and perhaps a little more pastis liqueur, to taste.

Garnish:
2 small fresh octopuses, fried
1 c (230 g) spider crab
2 boiled lobster tails
8 Norway lobsters
cherry tomatoes
fennel
dill
Rouille (saffron mayonnaise) (see page 246)

To make the garnish:
Buy ready-cleaned octopuses.
Cut the bodies into 0.4 inches (1 cm) thick rings and divide the arms in two.
Sear the octopuses very quickly in a hot pan.
Add salt and pepper.

If you buy the shellfish ready-cooked:
Cut up the shell with a pair of scissors, extract the meat and put it out in bowls before pouring the hot soup over it.

Skagen toast   serves 4

This is my version of by far the most popular appetizer
in Sweden, created by Tore Wretman some time in the 40s.
I have added a little chopped red (Spanish) onion, which
goes well with the bleak roe. Being a horseradish lover, I
throw that in as well.

   Note: Tore's toast was always made with fresh, hand-
peeled shrimp.

Ingredients:
2.2 lb (1 kg) fresh shrimp
⅔ c (160 mL) homemade mayonnaise (see page 245)
⅓ c (80 mL) crème fraîche
1 tsp (5 mL) Dijon mustard
1 bunch of dill, finely chopped
¼ red onion, minced
1 bunch of chives, finely chopped
4 slices of white bread with the crusts removed
2 tbsp (30 mL) butter for frying

Garnish:
¼ c (60 mL) Kalix bleak roe
a few sprigs of dill
freshly grated horseradish
salt and pepper

Procedure:
Peel the shrimp.
Mix the mayonnaise with the crème fraîche,
mustard, finely-chopped dill, red onion and chives.
Add salt and pepper.
Fry the bread in the butter until crisp and then
allow it to drain on paper towels.
Mix in the shrimp.
Arrange as illustrated, with the bleak roe.
Sprinkle with a little grated horseradish with a
little red onion and chives.
Beer and brännvin are the only possible drinks
for this one.

Mussel risotto with seared gambas
serves 4

The risotto has to be cooked in the mussel stock. And when the mussels are at their best, the risotto will be the same. It's great when you add seared gambas or shrimp. Note that the rice in the risotto must be al dente — shrimp and porridge? No thanks!

Serve with a good, ripe parmesan.

Ingredients:
2.2 lb (1 kg) blue mussels, washed and cleaned
¼ c (60 mL) dry white wine
12 fine gambas or Norway lobsters
½ c (115 g) coarsely-sliced, firm button mushrooms
  or good mushrooms of some other kind
2 shallots, finely chopped
1 clove of garlic
1 tbsp (15 mL) olive oil
⅔ c (160 mL) risotto rice (try to use either Arborio,
  Carnaroli or Vialone Nano rice)
2 c (480 mL) stock from cooking the mussels
2 tbsp (30 mL) butter
1 tbsp (15 mL) grated parmesan cheese
½ c (120 mL) whipping cream
salt and pepper

Garnish:
fresh basil

Procedure:
Discard any mussels that do not close up when gently tapped against the edge of the sink.
Cook the mussels in the wine in a covered saucepan until they have opened.
Discard any mussels that have not opened.
Save the stock.
Winkle out the mussels saving a few for garnish.
Stir-fry the mushrooms, onion and garlic in the oil.
Add the rice.
Dilute with the mussel stock a little at a time, and cook the risotto over a low heat until the rice feels soft, but still slightly al dente.
Stir in the butter, cheese and cream. Season to taste.
Sear the gambas and arrange as illustrated.

Mussel soup with pork and fennel

serves 4

A traditional shellfish recipe, and nowadays quite widespread. Mussels are now on sale in net bags in most places. Mussel farming is a booming business, and it is a good job to have.

I would like to raise a glass for mussels — the gold of the west coast of Sweden! The combination of mussels, parsley and lightly salted pork is outstanding. That's not to say I've forgotten about the garlic, of course …

Ingredients:
2.2 lb (1 kg) fresh blue mussels, thoroughly cleaned
¼ c (60 mL) olive oil
1 onion, minced
2 cloves of garlic, peeled and crushed
¾ c (180 mL) dry white wine
1¼ c (300 mL) whipping cream
1 bunch of plucked parsley
2 tbsp (30 mL) butter
3.5 oz (100 g) salt pork (white bacon), cut into strips
1 tbsp (15 mL) butter
1 small fennel bulb, finely grated
salt and pepper

Serve with:
½ c (120 mL) bread croutons

Garnish:
parsley

Procedure:
Heat the oil in a big saucepan.
Fry the onion and garlic in the oil without letting them change color.
Add the mussels, pour on the wine, stir and cover.
Boil for about 5 minutes, until the mussels open.
Remove the mussels with a slotted spoon and put aside for the time being.
Reduce the stock with the cream.
Pour the soup into a food processor, add the parsley and 2 tbsp (30 mL) butter and run until you have a smooth soup.
Season to taste.
Strain through a fine-meshed strainer.
Fry the pork until it is crispy and then allow it to drain on paper towels.
Heat 1 tbsp (15 mL) butter and put in the fennel, lightly fry.
Serve the soup in heated bowls with the pork, the mussels, bread croutons and fennel.
Garnish with parsley.

Garlic mussels
with hazelnut butter

serves 4

This recipe also works very well with snails. And if in the past you haven't been so keen on these shell-clad beauties, this is an excellent way to enjoy them. This butter, together with mussels or snails, is one of France's great culinary experiences.

Ingredients for cooking the mussels:
2.2 lb (1 kg) fresh blue mussels — cleaned, brushed
    and thoroughly rinsed
1 small bunch of parsley
1 shallot, peeled and chopped
2 cloves of garlic, peeled and chopped
1 tbsp (15 mL) butter
½ c (120 mL) dry white wine

Garlic mussel ingredients:
freshly cooked mussels
2 tbsp (30 mL) shallot, peeled and chopped
3 cloves of garlic, peeled and chopped
10 hazelnut kernels, chopped
⅔ c (150 g) butter at room temperature

Garnish:
spring onion, finely chopped

Serve with:
white bread

Procedure:
Discard all open mussels which do not close when
gently tapped.
Snap off the stalks of parsley.
Chop the leaves into small pieces and put them
aside for the moment.
Stir-fry the onion, garlic and parsley stalks in butter
in a saucepan for 2 minutes, without letting them
change color.
Pour in the wine, add the mussels, stir, cover
and cook for about 5 minutes, until the mussels open.
Remove the mussels from the saucepan.
Clean the mussels, remove the beard and put them a
side for the moment.
Set the oven to 440°F (225°C).
Mix the shallot, garlic, hazelnuts, butter and finely-
chopped parsley leaves together.
Put two mussels in each bowl and place them in
an oven-proof dish.
Butter the mussels.
Bake in the middle of the oven for 10 or 12 minutes
until the butter has melted and starts hissing.
Garnish with the finely-chopped spring onion
and serve with white bread.

Hint:
The mussel stock can be reduced and saved to use in a fish
recipe or mussel soup at another time.

Fusilli pasta with shellfish serves 4

Okay, I confess. I love Italy, I love pasta and I love shellfish.
So this recipe requires no explanation — just make, taste
and enjoy.

All it needs is a beautiful sunset!

Ingredients:
1 c (230 g) fusilli pasta, cooked as per the instructions
    on the package
2.2 lb (1 net or 1 kg) of clams, soft-shell clams
    or blue mussels, gutted and carefully cleaned
2 small lobsters, boiled and gutted
1 onion, minced
1 clove of garlic, chopped
2½ c (600 mL) olive oil
1 c (240 mL) whipping cream
½ c (115 g) fresh spinach
10 small vine tomatoes
½ c (115 g) grated parmesan cheese
salt and pepper

Procedure:
Fry the onion in the oil together with the garlic.
Put in the mussels and cook them until they open.
Remove half the mussels.
Pour in the cream and reduce for a few minutes.
Fold in the spinach and pasta, followed by the
remaining shellfish and the tomatoes.
Season to taste.
Transfer the pasta to a bowl and sprinkle with parmesan.
In Italy, they seldom serve parmesan with shellfish, but
I think it tastes very good!

Mussel soup with squash curry

serves 4

With its lime and lemon, this recipe has a bit of
a Thai touch.

Finish the dish off at the table by putting the squash
curry in bowls and pouring the soup over it as you serve.
Remember, all soup must be served piping hot, never
lukewarm!

Ingredients:
2.2 lb (1 net or 1 kg) of blue mussels,
    scrubbed and cleaned
2 shallots, peeled and finely chopped
4 cloves of garlic, peeled and minced
1 tbsp (15 mL) ginger, peeled and minced
2 stalks of lemongrass, sliced
butter for frying
juice of 2 limes
1⅔ c (400 mL) dry white wine
¾ c (180 mL) whipping cream
1 c (240 mL) coconut cream
salt and pepper

Squash curry:
½ c (115 g) squash (butternut, for example), peeled
    and diced
1 tbsp (15 mL) curry powder
1 chili — halved, de-seeded and finely chopped
butter for frying
3½ tbsp (50 mL) concentrated apple juice

Garnish:
blanched/lightly cooked squash cubes
parsley

Procedure:
Start with the squash curry:
Stir-fry the squash, curry powder and chili in the
butter without letting them change color, then add
the apple juice and cook for 5 minutes until the squash
softens.
Mix into a smooth purée in the mixer.
Check the mussels: tap them gently and make sure that
the open ones close up again. Discard any that don't.
Stir-fry the shallot, garlic, ginger and lemongrass
in the butter without their changing color.
Add the mussels, the juice from the limes and the wine.
Cover and simmer for 5 minutes.
Remove the mussels with a slotted spoon and put
them aside for the moment.
Add the cream and coconut cream to the stock.
Bring to a boil and season to taste.
Run the soup in the mixer until frothy.
Serve with the mussels and squash curry.
Garnish with squash cubes and parsley.

Clam chowder serves 4–6

It is considered sacrilegious to alter this wonderful American soup, but we feel like adding a little fish makes it extra satisfying. Monkfish fits the bill, being both firm-textured and outstandingly tasty.

Ingredients:
28 oz (800 g) fillet of monkfish, cleaned and trimmed (tusk loins or catfish will also do)
2.2 lb (1 kg) fresh blue mussels, rinsed and cleaned
1 lb (½ kg) cockles, rinsed and cleaned
1 onion, peeled and chopped
2 cloves of garlic, peeled and chopped
½ c (120 mL) minced bacon
1⅔ c (400 mL) dry white wine
1⅔ c (400 mL) water
fresh parsley stalks and sprigs of thyme
1 c (240 mL) diced squash (try butternut or Muscat)
½ small celeriac bulb, peeled and diced
2 large, firm potatoes, peeled and diced
2 c (480 mL) whipping cream
olive oil for frying

Garnish:
fried bread croutons
⅓ c (80 mL) plucked parsley and thyme leaves
fried slices of bacon

Procedure:
Set the oven to 330°F (165°C). Stir-fry the onion, garlic and bacon in a broad-bottomed saucepan.
Add the mussels, wine, water and herb stalks.
Cover and bring to a boil.
Stir thoroughly and bring to a boil again.
Remove the mussels with a slotted spoon and put them aside for the moment.
Reduce the liquid by about half.
Now add the squash, celeriac and potato.
Bring to a boil and add the cream.
Simmer over low heat for about 8 or 10 minutes, until the diced potato is soft but still slightly al dente.
Stir a few times with a wooden spoon.
Meanwhile, grill the fish in a pan until it is a nice color.
Transfer it to an oven-proof dish and insert an oven thermometer into the thickest part of the fish. Bake in the oven until the core temperature reaches 130–135°F (56–58°C).
Slice the fish.
Arrange the pot with the fish, plenty of mussels, bread croutons, a few extra slices of fried bacon and fresh herbs.

Asparagus wrapped in lardo with seared scallops and browned hazelnut butter serves 4

Fried or seared scallops never disappoint! Lardo
is Italian lard, well spiced. Which, together with
fried asparagus, means spicy, salty and delicious!

Ingredients:
8 lightly blanched stalks of white asparagus
4 lightly blanched stalks of green asparagus
12 thin slices of lardo
butter and oil for frying
12 scallops
salt and white pepper

Browned hazelnut butter:
¾ c (180 mL) browned butter
3½ tbsp (50 mL) soy sauce
½ c (115 g) hazelnuts — peeled, roasted
    and run through the mixer

Serve with:
2 tomatoes — halved, scooped out and cut up
spring mix salad leaves
French beans, halved

Procedure:
Start by lightly cooking the asparagus:
Put the soft butter into a warm frying pan
and heat it until golden brown.
Remove from the heat.
Reduce the soy sauce by half in a saucepan.
Add the hazelnuts and the browned butter.
Leave it to cook for a minute or so.
Wrap the green and white asparagus in lardo.
Fry it in butter and a little oil in a frying pan until
thoroughly soft — this will take about 3 minutes —
then season to taste with salt and fresh-milled
white pepper.
Season the scallops.
Fry them quickly, about 1 minute on each side, in
butter and oil over very high heat to give them a good
crisp surface.
Put out the asparagus and scallops on plates.
Drizzle with the reduced soy and garnish with
the tomatoes, salad leaves and French beans.

129

Yellow beet Carpaccio
with Norway lobster tails
and oyster and spinach sauce

serves 4

A fantastic mixture — Norway lobsters braised in white
wine, plus oyster and spinach sauce. Some may find the
combination a bit unusual, but with the appealing sauce
it's quite wonderful.

Remember that the yellow beets have to be cooked
just right, and their sweetness makes a good foil to the
salty tang of the Norway lobster.

Ingredients:
4 boiled yellow beets
12 raw Norway lobster tails
butter for frying

Oyster and spinach sauce:
4 opened oysters
about 1¾ oz (50 g) spinach, rinsed
⅓ c (80 mL) whipping cream

Garnish:
lemon zest
leaves of rosemary

Procedure:
Cut the yellow beets into thin slices.
Put these out, overlapping, onto four plates.
Combine the oysters, spinach and cream in the
mixer until you have a green sauce.
Fry the Norway lobster tails quickly in butter on
both sides, then add seasoning.
Place the Norway lobster tails on the slices of beet.
Heat the sauce carefully and serve separately.
Garnish with lemon zest and leaves of rosemary.

Mousseline of scallop and Norway lobster with truffle and Norway lobster sauce serves 4

This first-rate party recipe has relatively few ingredients and is therefore pretty easy to make, but remember when making the mixture that everything has to be thoroughly chilled.

This is a small, simple dish from the advanced French school, but it makes a great impression!

Ingredients:
½ c (115 g) meat of fresh scallops
4 large raw Norway lobster tails, peeled
½ c (120 mL) whipping cream
salt and pepper

Sauce:
1 c (240 mL) heavily reduced shellfish stock
    (see page 244)
¾ c (180 mL) whipping cream
1 small pat of butter
2 tsp (10 mL) truffle oil
salt and pepper

Garnish:
4 fresh scallops, removed from their shells
    and cleaned
1 small fresh or canned truffle
4 large raw Norway lobster tails, peeled

Procedure:
Set the oven to 200°F (95°C).
Combine the scallops in a food processor together with the cream, season to taste.
Half-fill an oven-proof dish with warm water.
Grease 4 oven-proof cocottes that are able to hold about 2 tsp (10 mL) each.
Put the mixture into the cocottes and push a Norway lobster into each of them.
Insert an oven thermometer into the middle of the mixture and bake in the middle of the oven until the core temperature is 140°F (60°C).
Reduce the (already reduced) shellfish stock with the cream until half remains.
Add a pat of butter, truffle oil and seasoning to taste.
Fry 4 Norway lobster tails and 4 scallops quickly in butter in a frying pan.
Beat or mix the sauce until it is frothy with a hand blender.
Serve the mousseline mixture with the fried shellfish, then pour the sauce over the dish and top it off with truffle shavings.

Fried lobster with lobster risotto

serves 4

I love Italian food, especially risotto, and this recipe is like a journey from Italy to Sweden.

Use the lobster shells to make the risotto stock. And remember, the rice in a risotto must be al dente!

Ingredients:
2 lobsters, pre-cooked and shelled (see page 249)
2 shallots, peeled and finely chopped
½ c (115 g) risotto rice (try to use either Arborio,
    Carnaroli or Vialone Nano rice)
butter for frying
⅓ c (80 mL) dry white wine
2 c (480 mL) lobster stock
2 tbsp (30 mL) butter
½ c (120 mL) grated parmesan

Garnish:
cherry tomatoes, boiled and peeled
fresh basil
arugula
olive oil flavored with basil

Procedure:
Fry the onion and rice in butter in a thick-bottomed
pan without letting them change color.
Add the wine and cook until the rice absorbs it.
Dilute with the stock, a little at a time, until the rice
is al dente; this will take about 15 minutes.
Stir in the butter and parmesan.
The risotto must be creamy when served; if it seems
too thick, add a little more stock.
Split the lobster tails down the middle.
Fry them with the lobster claws in butter in a frying pan.
Serve the lobster with the risotto.
Garnish with tomato, basil, arugula and basil-flavored
olive oil.

Lobster with a vanilla
beurre blanc sauce   serves 4

The first time I had shellfish with vanilla was at a restaurant in Dakar, Senegal. It was so good that in due course I served it at my restaurant on Gran Canaria.

People were a bit puzzled at first. "Who's the maniac trying to serve dessert with lobster? Oh well, might as well try it … Gosh, it's terrific!" We sold and served any amount.

Ingredients:
2 pre-cooked lobsters, about 1 lb (500 g) each
   (see page 249)
2 vanilla pods
the white of 2 leeks, cut into large rings
1 tbsp (15 mL) butter
1 batch of beurre blanc sauce (see page 247)
salt and pepper

Procedure:
Split the vanilla pods and scrape out the seeds.
Cut the lobsters into big pieces, using a sharp, strong knife.
Fry the pieces in butter with the leek.
Make the beurre blanc sauce and add vanilla to taste.
Season to taste.

Lobster Johanna serves 4

This dish was created by Crister Svantesson during his week as a guest chef at Hotel Reisen, Stockholm. During that week we served 2,160 lb (980 kg) of fresh lobster!

Please note, this recipe can only be made with female lobsters.

Ingredients:
2 medium-sized, pre-cooked lobsters (see page 249)
1 c (230 g) butter at room temperature
½ tbsp (7.5 mL) fresh tarragon, finely chopped
3 tbsp (45 mL) brandy
cayenne pepper
salt and pepper

Garnish:
fresh herbs

Procedure:
Set the oven to 440°F (225°C).
Split the lobsters, scrape out the halves, save the roe but discard the stomach.
Crack the claws.
Mix the butter, roe, tarragon and brandy together.
Season to taste, using salt, pepper and cayenne pepper.
Spread the lobster with the butter mixture and bake in the oven for about 25 minutes, until it has turned a nice color.
Garnish with fresh herbs.

140

Lobster in a sweet and sour dill sauce

serves 4

Here I'm harking back to classic Swedish home or country cooking. This is a tribute to the lobster fishermen of the Swedish province Bohuslän, who love sweet and sour sauce with their lobster. We should remember that once upon a time this was almost everyday fare!

Ingredients:
2 lobsters, boiled and shelled
12 young carrots, peeled
1 section of cabbage, cut in pieces
    (about 1 c or 230 g)
2 tbsp (30 mL) butter
4 tsp (20 mL) white wine sauce (see page 249)
2 tsp (10 mL) superfine sugar
2 tsp (10 mL) 12% proof distilled vinegar
3½ tbsp (50 mL) dill, finely chopped
salt and pepper

143

Garnish:
tufts of dill

Procedure:
Boil the carrots in a saucepan of water with butter
and salt until they soften.
Chill them directly in ice water to preserve their color.
Do the same with the cabbage; this takes about
2 minutes to cook.
Save the water in the saucepan.
Bring the white wine sauce to a boil in a saucepan.
Add sugar and vinegar to taste until the sauce is sweet
and sour.
Heat the lobster meat, carrots and cabbage carefully in
the vegetable cooking water and when done, arrange
them in a large bowl.
Froth up the sauce with a hand blender.
Now add the dill and pour the sauce over the lobster
and vegetables.

Lobster sausage with sauerkraut

makes 4 sausages

This one's a real humdinger! After all, what have we here if not the Rolls Royce of sausages? There's a touch of Alsatian inspiration here.

And the reward for your trouble? A taste of heaven after the very first mouthful.

Ingredients:
about 5 feet (1½ m) of hog casing (sausage skins)
3 cloves of garlic, roasted and minced
14 oz (400 g) scallop meat
¾ c (180 mL) whipping cream
7 oz (200 g) lobster meat, boiled and chopped
1¾ oz (50 g) ground lardo (Italian spiced lard)
    or pancetta
2 oz (59 g) sun-dried tomatoes, finely chopped
1 bunch of dill, finely chopped
3 anchovy fillets, finely chopped

Serve with:
warm sauerkraut
boiled potatoes
Dijon mustard (optional)

Procedure:
Put the casings to soak for about an hour before filling them.
Roast the garlic cloves in a frying pan or in the oven until they are soft and golden brown, then scoop them out.
Combine half of the scallop meat with the cream in a food processor to make a smooth mixture.
Chop up the remaining mussels into small pieces.
Combine all the ingredients into a smooth mixture.
Use a food processor with a sausage horn or else transfer the mixture to an icing bag with the nozzle removed. Stuff the casing with the mixture while carefully avoiding air bubbles.
Put the sausages into simmering water in a saucepan. The water temperature must be 175°F (80°C); check this with a thermometer.
Alternatively, fry the sausages in butter in a frying pan. The sausages are ready when they feel rigid and the c ore temperature is at least 130°F (55°C). Check this by inserting a roasting thermometer into the middle of a sausage.
Serve with warm sauerkraut, boiled potatoes and perhaps a little Dijon mustard.

144

Smørrebrød with smoked shrimp

serves 4

A smørrebrød is a Danish open sandwich. I love Denmark
and go there as often as I can. While there, I'll visit a well-
known smørrebrød restaurant, and have a splendid lunch
of three or four open sandwiches.

   With it, of course, one relishes a cool lager. Or two. Or
more, if I'm traveling with Erik Lallerstedt.

Ingredients:
2.2 lb (1 kg) boiled shrimp
1 tsp (5 mL) curry powder
a pat of butter for frying
¼ c (60 mL) crème fraîche
½ onion, finely chopped
1 apple, finely minced
10–12 cold boiled potatoes, sliced
4 slices of Danish rye bread
salt and pepper

Garnish:
½ onion, cut into rings
1 small carrot, finely grated
a few thin slices of apple
chervil

Procedure:
Fry the curry in the butter in a frying pan, then
leave it to cool.
Mix the crème fraîche with the curry, butter,
onion and apple.
Season to taste.
Lastly, fold in the potato.
Put aside for the moment.
Peel the shrimp.
Arrange the potato salad and shrimp on the rye bread.
Garnish with onion rings, strips of carrot, thin slices
of apple and chervil.

Fish 'n chips with Norway lobster and a lobster and fennel aïoli

serves 4

I'm fascinated by this English fast-food classic that you can eat on the street out of newspaper or in the pub.

The following is a classic dish that has been enhanced by using Norway lobsters and served with homemade, wafer-thin chips (which are delicious when salted!).

Ingredients:
20 raw Norway lobster tails, peeled
6 firm potatoes, cut in thin slices
cooking oil for deep frying
flour
salt and fresh-milled white pepper

Batter:
⅔ c (150 mL) rice flour
3½ tbsp (50 mL) white flour
1¼ c (300 mL) beer or mineral water
3 egg whites
juice of 1 lemon
salt

Serve with:
lobster and fennel aïoli (see page 245)

Garnish:
lemon wedges
salad shoots
onion rings

Procedure:
Rinse the sliced potatoes until the starch is gone.
Let them dry on a paper towel.
Deep-fry them a few at a time in an oiled, wide-bottomed saucepan until they are crisp and golden brown.
Add salt to taste.
Mix the rice flour, white flour and a little salt together in a bowl.
Stir in the beer or mineral water, a little at a time. You want the batter to be as smooth and creamy as possible.
Beat the egg whites until fluffy with the lemon juice.
Stir one-third of the beaten egg whites into the beer and flour mixture.
Now carefully fold in the remaining egg whites.
Season the Norway lobsters with salt and fresh-milled white pepper.
Dredge them in flour and dip them in the batter.
Deep-fry in oil at 355°F (180°C) until they are crisp and golden brown.
Add salt to taste.
Serve the Norway lobster tails with the lobster and fennel aïoli. Garnish with lemon wedges, salad shoots and onion rings.

148

Hint:
Check the oil temperature with a thermometer or a piece of white bread. Turn off the cooker fan and keep a lid handy in case the oil starts to splash.

Boiling freshwater crayfish

This recipe is for boiling fresh freshwater crayfish such as signal crayfish and the *Astacus astacus* (also known as European crayfish, the noble crayfish or the broad-fingered crayfish). They should be rinsed before cooking to get rid of any bait residue.

Killing the crayfish
Fill a broad-bottomed saucepan three-quarters full with unsalted water. When the water is boiling fiercely, immerse between 6 and 10 crayfish at a time for just over a minute. Kill them like this in relays.

Boiling
Having killed all the crayfish, prepare the cooking stock which should be kept boiling for about 15 minutes before the crayfish are added to it.
Cook the crayfish for about 5 minutes after the water has come to a boil again. Leave them to cool in their juices.

Cooking liquid ingredients for 2.2 lb (1 kg) crayfish:
2.64 quarts (2½ L) of water
5 tbsp (75 mL) coarse salt, or 4 tbsp (60 mL) fine salt
1 tsp (5 mL) sugar
plenty of dill crowns
½ c (120 mL) beer or stout (optional)

(If you're buying frozen crayfish, this stock will improve their flavor. Boil the stock, let it cool slightly and then put in the crayfish while they are still frozen. Store in the fridge for 12 hours or, better still, for 24.)

Cold roast veal
with signal crayfish serves 4

Meat and crayfish make an exciting combination —
fantastically so! The pure, pale meaty flavor of the
cold roast veal goes very well with the crayfish tails.

   If you don't have crayfish tails, gambas or shrimp
will do.

Ingredients:
1.3 lb (about 21 oz or 600 g) thin slices of cold roast veal
1 small jar of capers (about 1¾ oz or 50 g)
1 bunch of basil
3½ tbsp (50 g) roasted pine nuts
1¾ oz (50 g) shavings of Manchego cheese
20 signal crayfish, peeled and boiled
salt and pepper

Procedure:
Arrange all the ingredients on a big serving dish
or four plates.
Serve with a fresh green salad and a cold herb sauce.

Globe artichoke crowns (bottoms) stuffed with signal crayfish   serves 4

When it's crayfish-party time, buy a few extra pounds and serve the crayfish warm and, in this case, on globe artichoke crowns. There are exciting ways of eating crayfish other than with dill and cheese!

Ingredients:
4 fresh globe artichoke crowns
40 boiled signal crayfish
2 c (480 mL) water
1 lemon
3½ tbsp (50 mL) superfine sugar
salt and pepper

Crayfish sauce:
the shells of the 40 crayfish
¾ c (180 mL) onion, peeled and chopped
⅓ c (80 mL) carrot, peeled and chopped
⅓ c (80 mL) celeriac, peeled and chopped
⅓ c (80 mL) parsnip, peeled and chopped
¼ c (60 mL) tomato purée
oil for frying
2 cloves of garlic, peeled and crushed
4 crown dill crowns
½ tbsp (7.5 mL) dried thyme
1 tbsp (15 mL) paprika powder
2 bay leaves
2 c (480 mL) whipping cream
⅓ c (80 mL) Madeira
3½ tbsp (50 mL) eau de vie (clear, colorless fruit brandy)

Garnish:
globe artichoke stalks
perhaps a whole cooked globe artichoke
crayfish shells
tufts of dill

Procedure:
The sauce:
Set the oven to 390°F (200°C).
Peel the crayfish and store them in the fridge for the time being.
Rinse the shells in a colander to get rid of some of the salt.
Spread them out on a baking sheet and roast them in the middle of the oven for about 25 minutes.

Meanwhile, stir-fry the vegetables and tomato purée in the oil in a wide-bottomed saucepan.
Add the roasted crayfish shells, the garlic and the spices.
Pour on enough water to cover. Bring to a boil and simmer for about 40 minutes.
Strain through a fine-meshed strainer and reduce the liquid until about 1⅔ c (400 mL) remains.
Add the cream, the Madeira and eau de vie and cook the sauce for a few minutes.
Season to taste.

The globe artichokes:
Snap off the shafts of the globe artichokes by holding them firmly against a cutting board and pressing down with the palm of your hand.
Trim the artichoke crowns with a sharp knife, removing all the green. The "heart" inside will be removed later.
Cut away the green, woody outer casing from the stalks.
After cleaning each globe artichoke, put it in cold water with a little acid — lemon or vinegar, for example — to prevent discoloration.
Bring the water to a boil in a wide-bottomed saucepan.
Add the lemon juice, sugar and a little salt.
Add the lemon peel for the last minute or two, then remove them with a slotted spoon and discard.
Check the flavor of the water until you have a pleasing balance between salty, sour and sweet.
Put in the globe artichoke crowns and the stalks.
Cook them for about an hour.
They are ready when the heart comes away from the crown easily.
The stalks will be ready first. Remove them with a slotted spoon as soon as they have softened.
Put them on a plate to cool and then remove the heart with a spoon; save the cooking liquid.
When the globe artichokes are ready, heat them in the stock.
Fill them with the crayfish and pour the sauce over them.
Garnish with the globe artichoke stalks, crayfish shells and tufts of dill.
I recommend cooking an extra globe artichoke and keeping it whole. Its leaves will then make a tasty spoon for scooping up the last of the sauce.

Poached chicken with signal crayfish and Västerbotten cheese serves 4

You might think that this is a strange combination, but it's common in France, especially in the region of Grenoble where they're great crayfish eaters.

The sauce contains Västerbotten cheese and the delicate, pale chicken meat blends nicely with the crayfish — une marriage formidable!

Ingredients:
1 large whole chicken or two smaller ones
30–40 signal crayfish, boiled and shelled
8 small onions, peeled
4 carrots
1 tbsp (15 mL) dill seeds
2 bay leaves
5 white peppercorns
4¼ c (1 L) chicken stock (see page 244)
1 c (240 mL) whipping cream
½ c (115 g) grated Västerbotten cheese
1 bunch of dill, finely chopped

Procedure:
Put the chicken, onion, carrots and herbs into a big casserole dish.
Pour on the stock.
Bring to a boil and cook gently for 30 or 40 minutes, until the chicken is done.
Test the chicken with a skewer to make sure the juices run clear.
Meanwhile, peel the crayfish (and why not save the shells for stock?).
Remove the chicken and vegetables with a slotted spoon.
Reduce the stock until it's really flavorful.
Add the cream and reduce slightly.
Froth up the sauce with a hand blender.
Mix in the cheese and dill.
Carve the chicken.
Serve with the vegetables, crayfish tails and sauce.
Mashed potatoes make a good accompaniment.

American shrimp cocktail serves 4

For this recipe, use the biggest shrimp you can get. (Standing in front of American fish counters, you're really spoiled for choice — every conceivable size, boiled, raw, smoked ... Browsing is a heavenly experience in itself.)

The first time I had this sauce, I thought it was shocking. Now I love it, and gladly eat it with oysters, crab — in fact, any shellfish whatsoever.

Ingredients:
plenty of large boiled shrimp
1 bunch of celery

Serve with:
cocktail sauce (see page 247)

Procedure:
Peel the shrimp without removing the very end of the tail. Serve as illustrated, on the rocks and with cocktail sauce.

159

Asian lobster salad serves 4

Fresh, just-cooked lobster, mango and coriander —
an unbeatable combination. And don't shy away from
using spice: this dish has to be a little on the hot side.

Use the tail and the claws — both delicious and
highly decorative!

Ingredients:
2 boiled lobsters (about 1 lb or 500 g each)
4 ripe mangos, peeled and diced
1 red chili, finely chopped
10 leaves of fresh coriander, chopped
1 tbsp (15 mL) olive oil
grated zest of 2 limes
1 bunch of lollo rosso lettuce, rinsed
    and plucked in small pieces
salt and pepper

Garnish:
10 whole plucked leaves of fresh coriander

Procedure:
Shell and clean the lobsters, split the tails down the
middle and remove the gut running the length of them.
Mix the mango, chili, coriander, olive oil and lime
peel together.
Add salt and pepper.
Put out the mixture on four plates.
Put a few lettuce leaves, ½ lobster tail and 1 claw
on each plate.
Garnish with coriander leaves.

Oysters au gratin cooked in porter

serves 4

Au gratin is a good way of serving oysters to the unconvinced. They'll fall for them! The important thing is to serve the oysters immediately, while they're warm.

Ingredients:
20 Swedish oysters, opened and removed from their shells
1 bunch of dill
1 bottle of dark porter (stout), about 1½ c (330 mL)
1 banana shallot, peeled and chopped
3 egg yolks
juice of 1 lemon
1⅓ c (310 mL) lukewarm clarified butter
3½ tbsp (50 mL) lukewarm browned butter
2 tbsp (30 mL) whipped cream
salt and fresh-milled white pepper

Garnish:
deep-fried leek
1 tomato, halved, scooped out and cut in pieces
parsley

Procedure:
Pluck the dill in neat sprigs and chop finely.
Save the stalks.
Pour the porter into a saucepan.
Add the dill stalks and banana shallot.
Bring to a boil and reduce to ¼ c (60 mL).
Strain the reduced liquid and leave to cool completely.
Place the egg yolks in a heavy-bottomed saucepan.
Beat the egg yolks, porter reduction, lemon juice
and a little salt together.
Simmer gently, whisking continuously until
the mixture is smooth, thick and creamy.
Beat in the clarified butter and the browned butter,
a drop at a time.
Fold the whipped cream and chopped dill into
the mixture.
Season to taste with salt and fresh-milled white pepper.
Set the oven to 480°F (250°C).
Place the oysters on a bed of coarse salt in
an oven-proof dish.
Put roughly a tablespoon of the porter hollandaise
on each oyster (enough to cover it).
Bake at the top of the oven for about 2 minutes, until
the oysters are a nice color.
Shred and deep-fry the leek.
Garnish with the deep-fried leek, bits of tomato and parsley.

Cocktail with grilled oysters and smoked pork serves 4

With oysters and pork you can never go wrong!
Grilling the oysters brings out a splendid salty tang
which goes very well with the pork. Peas are good
for you, and everyone should eat more of them.

So make this cocktail frequently — it's worth it!

Ingredients:
8 oysters, removed from their shells
8 medium-sized almond potatoes, peeled
3½ tbsp (50 g) butter at room temperature
⅓ c (80 mL) whipping cream
a little warm milk (optional)
1 c (230 g) small green peas
melted butter
5¼ oz (150 g) smoked pork, cut in large pieces
salt and pepper

Garnish:
1 sprig of dill

Procedure:
Boil the potatoes.
Rice them into a bowl through a potato ricer.
Beat in the butter and cream.
Season to taste.
Add, if you like, a little warm milk for a
creamy consistency.
Mash the peas in a little melted butter, season to taste.
Grill the pork on all sides in a really hot frying pan,
to give it a nice color.
Quickly grill the oysters on both sides in the pork fat
and in the same frying pan.
Put the potato mixture into cocktail glasses.
Put the peas and pork on top, followed by the oysters.
Garnish with dill.

Oyster pie with crispy bacon

serves 4

A bloody good recipe, if you'll pardon my French. Should
you ever find yourself with a few tubs (boxes, bags …)
of oysters to spare, try this recipe. Warm oysters are one of
my favorites, and the crispy bacon completes the dish.

Ingredients:
18 fresh oysters, newly opened, laid on a paper towel
14 oz (400 g) ready-made dough
1 leek, finely minced
½ tbsp (7.5 mL) butter
1 bunch of dill, finely chopped
3 eggs
1 c (240 mL) whipping cream
7 oz (200 g) Västerbotten cheese
salt and pepper

Garnish:
7 oz (200 g) fried bacon
fresh basil

Procedure:
Set the oven to 480°F (250°C).
Line a pie pan with a thin layer of dough and bake slightly.
Lower the oven temperature to 390°F (200°C).
Fry the leek in the butter.
Add seasoning and place the leek on the
bottom of the pan.
Put in the oysters and sprinkle the dill over them.
Beat the eggs and cream together and pour
the mixture into the pan.
Add the cheese.
Bake in the oven for 20 or 25 minutes.
Top with fried bacon and a little fresh basil.

Poached oysters with spinach and hollandaise on toast serves 4

This is a pleasant way of cooking oysters, and poached oysters make a good appetizer or a late-night bite. They can also be served as a better class of snack, together with a crisp champagne. Taste buds will burst into song!

Ingredients:
4 oysters, removed from their shells
2 egg yolks
1–2 tsp (5–10 mL) lemon juice
1 tbsp (15 mL) water
¾ c (180 mL) melted butter
white bread, cut into 4 round or triangular slices
1 package (3½ oz or 100 g) of baby spinach
salt and pepper

Garnish:
1½ oz (43 g) bleak roe
1 sprig of dill

Procedure:
Beat the egg yolks in a mixing bowl over a water bath together with the water, a little salt and 1 tsp (5 mL) pressed lemon juice, until the mixture thickens and turns creamy.
Melt the butter and leave aside until it's about 140°F (60°C).
Add the melted butter in a thin jet, whisking continuously. If you like, season with more pressed lemon juice and salt and pepper. Set aside for the moment.
Fry the bread golden brown on both sides in butter.
Set aside and keep warm.
Fry the spinach quickly in a little butter.
Add seasoning.
Poach the oyster meat for 10 or 20 seconds in lightly salted water.
Remove and drain.
Put spinach and oysters on the fried bread.
Spread the hollandaise sauce on top.
Top off with bleak roe and a small sprig of dill.

Crab au gratin
with Swedish anchovies

serves 4

Crab au gratin is a real treat, and when you serve it in the shell, you also get you a new plate!

You must try to use real Swedish anchovy fillets made with sprats because they simply melt into the au gratin.

Ingredients:
4 fat crabs, females if possible
2 tbsp (30 mL) butter
½ tbsp (7.5 mL) flour
1¼ c (300 mL) whipping cream
½ c (120 mL) shellfish stock (see page 244)
8 Swedish anchovy fillets
¼ c (60 mL) strong cheese (Västerbotten if possible),
   grated
salt and pepper

Procedure:
Wash the crabs and boil them for 15 or 20 minutes.
Leave them to cool in the liquid.
Set the oven to 480°F (250°C).
Extract the crab meat and save the shells, after drying them well.
Cut the crab meat into large pieces.
Melt the butter in a saucepan.
Whisk in the flour.
Add the cream and shellfish stock.
Reduce to a thick sauce, whisking continuously.
Carefully fold in the crab meat.
Season to taste.
Fill the shells with the mixture and top each helping with 2 anchovy fillets.
Sprinkle with the cheese and bake in the middle of the oven for 3 or 4 minutes.
Serve warm as a late-night snack or a starter.

Crab salad   serves 4

When making this kind of salad, it's a good idea to use a
mold or cocotte so that you can arrange the ingredients in
layers. The recipe does not have to be followed exactly:
use whatever shellfish are around, depending on what
you've caught, found on special or is looking extra fresh
and tasty at the supermarket.

Ingredients:
2 fat female crabs
1 package of arugula
4 tomatoes, diced
½ cucumber, diced
½ c (115 g) lightly cooked runner beans, minced
½ c (120 mL) Dijon vinaigrette (see page 246)
¼ c (60 mL) trout roe

Procedure :
Clean and shell the crabs, keeping the meat as
intact as possible.
Arrange the arugula, crab meat and vegetables with
the Dijon vinaigrette in layers as illustrated.
Serve with trout roe and mustard sauce (see page 248).

Warm crab claws

The inspiration for this recipe came from America. In
Miami there is a famous restaurant called Joe's Stone
Crab where they serve crab claws, and once the crab
season is underway you can't get a table there for love or
money.

Stone crabs are farmed in Miami and their claws are
harvested alternately (the left and then the right, or vice
versa). In between harvests you just wait for new claws to
grow again.

The claws are served with good sauces, but always with
melted butter.

Procedure:
Serve freshly boiled crabs with clarified butter, fresh-
baked bread and — I recommend — other sauces like
chili mayonnaise or mustard mayonnaise (see page 245).

Crab bruschetta as a starter

4 small helpings

Not just any old sandwich, but an Italian sandwich. This is a great sandwich for in front of the television, while watching that crucial game — the kind of occasion when only the best is good enough.

Ingredients:
16 crab claws
butter for frying
4 slices of white bread (day-old if possible)

Tomato concassé:
1 can of crushed tomatoes
½ c (120 mL) onion, peeled and finely chopped
olive oil for frying
2 tbsp (30 mL) white balsamic vinegar
1 tbsp (15 mL) Demerara sugar
1 tbsp (15 mL) crown (or ordinary) dill, chopped
1 tbsp (15 mL) basil, chopped
salt and pepper

Garnish:
dill sprigs
a slice of lemon
parmesan shavings

Procedure:
Start with the tomato concassé:
Pour the tomatoes into a strainer, to get rid of extra liquid (though you can very well save it for another time). While the tomatoes are draining, shell the crab claws carefully and remove the cartilage inside each claw with a small, sharp knife.
Put the claws aside.
Fry the onion in olive oil in a saucepan for about 2 minutes until it is nice and shiny.
Add the strained tomatoes, balsamic vinegar and Demerara sugar.
Simmer gently for about 25 minutes, stirring occasionally from the bottom.
Finish off with the herbs and season to taste.
Remove from the heat and leave to cool.
Melt the butter in a small saucepan and put in the crab claws.
Fry the slices of bread golden brown in plenty of olive oil.
Put both the crab claws and the slices of bread to drain on a paper towel.
Spread the tomato concassé on the slices of bread and put the crab meat on top.
Finish off with parmesan shavings, slices of lemon and sprigs of dill.

Spider crab with an avocado dressing serves 4

The spider crab is much bigger than the name sounds, and the species is rapidly spreading southwards from the Bering Sea — however, it's not spreading fast enough for me, because I consider it to be a real delicacy.

Enjoy it as it is or with salsa. It's incredibly good, but it's also improved by grilling. The best raw materials are like that — there are many different ways of treating them, with different flavorings and in different recipes, but of course they're wonderful just as they are.

Ingredients:
8 large spider crabs, boiled and split
2 ripe avocados, diced
⅓ c (80 mL) olive oil
1 crushed clove of garlic
2 tbsp (30 mL) sweet chili sauce
1 tbsp (15 mL) fresh coriander, coarsely chopped
salt and pepper

Garnish:
fresh coriander

Procedure:
Mix all the dressing ingredients together
and then pour the dressing over the crabs.
Garnish with a little fresh coriander.

Asian shore crab soup serves 4

This recipe forms the base of a reduced stock and provides us with another recipe.

Many people love Thai food, and it is indeed a new culinary trend. One should remember that Thai food is easy to prepare: all you have to do is make sure to have the basic ingredients (such as a jar of curry paste, dried lime leaves and fish sauce) at home.

And don't be shy about flavoring. The result needs to be a little on the hot side!

Stock ingredients:
1.1 lb (½ kg) whole, live shore crabs
2 cloves of garlic
2 stalks of lemongrass
1 piece of fresh ginger (about the size of your thumb)
1 tbsp (15 mL) cooking oil
1 pimiento, coarsely chopped
1 shallot, coarsely chopped
1 tbsp (15 mL) tomato purée
4¼ c (1 L) of water
½ c (120 mL) lemon juice
½ c (120 mL) Asian fish sauce

Serve with:
12 shelled crab claws
5 segmented button mushrooms
8 thin slices of King Solo (or jumbo) garlic
1 stalk of lemongrass (only the thicker part), finely grated
1 tbsp (15 mL) ginger, finely grated
1 tsp (5 mL) pimiento, minced
chives

Procedure:
Begin by roughly crushing the crabs with the back of a pan or the handle of a knife.
Now crush the garlic, lemongrass and ginger in a mortar.
Heat a wide-bottomed saucepan and pour in a little cooking oil.
Stir-fry the crabs, the crushed herbs, the chili and the shallot over high heat for about 2 minutes.
Add the tomato purée and stir-fry for another minute.
Pour on the water, lemon juice and fish sauce.
Bring to a boil and then simmer for about 15 minutes.
Strain into another saucepan.
Add the button mushrooms and bring them to a boil.
Put in the crab claws and spices.

Scallops with pata negra ham, root parsley purée and balsamic vinaigrette serves 4

This recipe was inspired by flavors I experienced in Barcelona. The pata negra ham from the black-footed Spanish pig and the fresh sun-ripened figs are a classic combination.

And then the porcini (*Boletus edulis*) and scallops!
This starter is a Sjömagasinet classic.

Ingredients:
8 scallops
4 slices of pata egra ham

Root parsley purée ingredients:
½ c (115 g) root parsley, peeled and diced
½ c (120 mL) whipping cream
⅓ c (80 mL) milk
1 small bunch of parsley
salt and pepper

Balsamic vinaigrette ingredients:
½ c (120 mL) balsamic vinegar
1 tbsp (15 mL) superfine sugar
3½ tbsp (50 mL) sultanas
3½ tbsp (50 mL) olive oil

Garnish:
12 porcini, fried and halved
4 fresh figs, segmented
pea shoots

Procedure:
Bring the cream and milk for the purée to
a boil in a saucepan.
Add the root parsley and cook for 10 minutes
until it softens.
Strain off the cream and milk mixture, but save it.
Mix the root parsley with the leaf parsley, dilute
with the cream and milk mixture to the right consistency.
Season to taste.
Reduce the balsamic vinegar and the sugar in a
saucepan until half remains, add the sultanas, leave
to cool and then mix with the olive oil.
Fry the scallops quickly on both sides in butter in
a frying pan, then salt and pepper them.
Put out the ham, scallops and root parsley purée
and drizzle with the vinaigrette.

Caesar salad
with Norway lobster tails serves 4

Caesar is the king of salads, with wonderful possibilities.
Here we have the classic salad with seared Norway lobster
tails, but consider adding other delicious ingredients —
your imagination's the limit!

Ingredients:
2 heads of romaine lettuce
12 raw Norway lobster tails, halved
3 egg yolks
2 tsp (10 mL) Dijon mustard
1 clove of garlic, peeled and crushed
1 tbsp (15 mL) capers, chopped
4–6 Italian sardel anchovy fillets, chopped
¾ c (180 mL) olive oil
2 tbsp (30 mL) parmesan cheese, finely grated
salt (optional)
black pepper

Serve with:
½ c (120 mL) bread croutons
½ c (120 mL) parmesan cheese, coarsely grated

Procedure:
Mix the egg yolks, mustard, garlic, capers
and anchovies together.
Beat in the olive oil and add the parmesan cheese.
Season to taste with salt and black pepper.
Break up the lettuce into smaller pieces. Rinse them
and dry them carefully.
Mix the lettuce into the dressing.
Season the Norway lobster tails.
Sear them for about 2 minutes in a frying pan.
Arrange the salad on plates, garnish with the Norway
lobster tails and sprinkle with the parmesan cheese
and bread croutons.

Pancetta-wrapped scallop
with sage

serves 4

Talk about an Italian dream! The smokiness of the pancetta and the sage blend nicely with the pure shellfish taste of the scallop. Just the thing for watching Italian soccer on television!

I've been in Italy quite a lot, and it's a fantastic country. Try driving there and just meandering around for 10 days or two weeks, eating, drinking and enjoying life to the fullest.

Ingredients:
12 scallops
12 slices of pancetta
12 sage leaves
½ c (115 g) polenta
3½ tbsp (50 mL) grated parmesan
4¼ tsp (20 g) butter
juice and grated zest of 1 lemon
butter for frying
salt and pepper

Garnish:
sage leaves
parmesan shavings
grated lemon peel

Procedure:
Put out the pancetta on a cutting board.
Put one sage leaf on each slice of ham.
Add a scallop and roll up; secure with a toothpick.
Cook the polenta as per the instructions on the package.
When it's done, beat in grated parmesan, butter, lemon peel and lemon juice.
The consistency has to be creamy.
Season to taste.
Quickly fry the scallops in butter in a frying pan for about 1–2 minutes per side until they are a nice color.
Spoon out the polenta on plates.
Spread the scallops on top.
Garnish with sage leaves, parmesan and lemon peel.
Serve immediately.

Roquefort-baked
Norway lobsters

serves 4

Most recipes for Norway lobster au gratin come from the
Tenan ("Lobster Pot") restaurant in Marstrand, on the
west coast of Sweden.

Here's a variant that uses Roquefort cheese, which
spreads a wonderful fragrance through the kitchen and the
dining room. The salty tang of the cheese is an ideal
accompaniment to the fine flavor of the Norway lobsters.

Ingredients:
8 large Norway lobsters, preferably raw, split
	and with gut and stomach removed
7 oz (200 g) genuine Roquefort cheese, coarsely grated
1 bunch of parsley, coarsely chopped
2 crushed cloves of garlic
½ c (120 mL) crème fraîche
½ c (120 mL) olive oil
½ c (120 mL) dry white wine
salt and pepper

Procedure:
Set the oven to 440°F (225°C).
Put the Norway lobster halves onto a big oven-proof dish.
Mix the cheese and other ingredients together in a
food processor.
Season to taste.
Pour the dressing over the Norway lobsters and bake
in the middle of the oven for about 10–12 minutes, until
they change color.
Serve instantly with warm bread.

Lemon-splashed Norway lobsters with paprika salad   serves 4

This recipe reminds me of Barcelona. The idea for this combination came to me while visiting and temporarily working there.

In this dish of pre-cooked, lemon-splashed Norway lobsters, the summery sharpness of lemon counters the sweetness of the roasted paprika. Not only delicious, but good for you!

Ingredients:
12 Norway lobsters, pre-cooked and peeled (see page 249)
2 red paprikas
2 yellow paprikas
olive oil
2 shallots, finely chopped
butter
2 lemons
salt and pepper

Garnish:
rosemary
lemon zest
onion

Procedure:
Set the oven to 480°F (250°C).
Halve the paprikas and de-core them.
Rub the shells with a little olive oil and put them
on a baking sheet lined with parchment paper.
Remove the paprikas when they are a deep color
and the skin has started to come away.
Cool in an ice bath.
Peel and dice the paprikas.
Sauté the shallot in olive oil and butter
without it changing color.
Put in the Norway lobsters and squeeze
the lemons over them.
Simmer gently for about 2 minutes.
Season to taste.

Norway lobster Carpaccio
with beets marinated in truffle oil

serves 4

I love Carpaccio in any shape or form, but I think it's
really at its best with Norway lobsters. The mild flavor
of the crayfish meat, the truffle …
    This one will really wow them.

Ingredients:
8 Norway lobster tails, pre-cooked and peeled
    (see page 249)
4 boiled beets
¼ c (60 mL) truffle oil
¼ c (60 mL) white wine vinegar
salt and pepper

Garnish:
arugula
parmesan cheese
herb shoots

204

Procedure:
Place the Norway lobster tails on a sheet of folded
plastic foil, put another sheet on top and hammer the
tails flat with a rolling pin or other heavy instrument.
Store the whole thing in the freezer until the
tails are frozen.
Put out on a plate and trim to size.
Cut the beets into segments.
Turn these in the truffle oil and white wine vinegar.
Season to taste.
Place the beets on the Norway lobster Carpaccio.
Drizzle the Norway lobster tails with truffle oil
and the vinegar from the beets.
Garnish with arugula and parmesan.

Norway lobster salad with avocado and blood grapefruit   serves 4

The freshness of it! Try asking for an extra sweet grapefruit. The acidity makes an admirable foil to the Norway lobsters. And the mild flavor of the avocado makes a good foundation for this wonderful salad, which is just the thing for a dinner party or a side dish.

Ingredients:
12 Norway lobsters, boiled and peeled
2 avocados, peeled, with the pit removed
1 blood grapefruit, peeled and filleted
    (squeeze out the juice and save)
1½ oz (43 g) trout roe
1 bunch of fresh tarragon
salt and pepper

Procedure:
Scoop out the avocado flesh and mash it
together with the grapefruit juice.
Add salt and pepper.
Put out the avocado mixture on plates.
Shape it in a mold.
Place the Norway lobsters, fillets of grapefruit
and trout roe on top.
Garnish with tarragon leaves.

Norway lobster with Baltic herring

serves 4

You can never go wrong combining crayfish and Baltic
herring, but using Norway lobsters instead of crayfish
is like graduating from a T-Ford to a Rolls Royce!
This really is something to write home about.

Ingredients:
12 double fillets of Baltic herring,
    with the dorsal fins removed
12 raw Norway lobster tails, peeled
1 tbsp (15 mL) tomato purée
½ c (120 mL) tomato juice
3½ tbsp (50 mL) olive oil
1 tsp (5 mL) crushed dill seeds
2 tbsp (30 mL) Swedish anchovy liquor
1 bunch of dill, chopped
butter for the oven dish
salt and pepper

Garnish:
sprigs of dill

Procedure:
Mix the tomato purée, tomato juice, olive oil,
dill seeds and anchovy liquor together in a
mixing bowl.
Put in the Baltic herring fillets and turn them
in the mixture.
Set the oven to 320°F (160°C).
Roll each Norway lobster tail in chopped dill.
Place the Baltic herring fillets skin side up.
Season them and put one Norway lobster on each.
Roll them up and transfer to an oven-proof dish.
Bake in the middle of the oven for 20 minutes.
Store in the fridge, overnight if possible.
Halve them and garnish with dill.

Sea urchin soup serves 4

A somewhat unusual raw material, but sea urchins are
sold in well-stocked specialty fish stores, and if not, you
can always try to order them. My love of sea urchins has
not always been requited.

   While in Spain, I was once out swimming when a big
wave swept me in against the pier, where I collided with an
entire colony of sea urchins. I was picking spines out of my
leg for months! After that I didn't eat sea urchins quite as
often, but they're still a delicacy.

Ingredients:
3½ oz (100 g) sea urchin roe
   (order from a specialty fish store or supermarket)
3 shallots, peeled and finely chopped
butter for frying
½ bottle dry white wine
2 c (480 mL) good fish stock (see page 244)
1¼ c (300 mL) milk
1¼ c (300 mL) whipping cream
3½ tbsp (50 g) butter at room temperature
2 tbsp (30 mL) crème fraîche
1 tbsp (15 mL) good white wine vinegar
salt and pepper

Garnish:
thyme

Serve with:
freshly-baked bread

Procedure:
Fry the onion in butter in a big saucepan,
without allowing it to change color.
Pour on the wine and stock and reduce to about half.
Add the milk and cream and reduce a little further.
Beat in the butter and crème fraîche.
Add seasoning and white wine vinegar to taste.
Mix in the roe with a hand blender, then strain.
Garnish with the thyme.
Serve in hot bowls with freshly-baked bread.

Toast fried in butter with a Brie, lobster and truffle cream filling
makes about 10 snack servings

When you boil or make something with lobster there will usually be a little meat left over (if not, it can be arranged!). Lobster and the mushroom taste of Brie are well matched indeed.

Instead of lobster, you can use shrimp or Norway lobster meat. This toast goes very well with soup, or else as part of a buffet or a supper dish.

Ingredients:
8¾ oz (250 g) Brie du pays
flesh of 1 lobster
1 tbsp (15 mL) truffle oil
7 oz (200 g) cream cheese
20 slices of white bread with the crusts removed
butter for frying

Garnish:
one or two fresh truffle shavings (optional)
mint leaves

Procedure:
Mix the Brie, lobster meat, truffle oil and cream cheese together, using either a whisk or a food processor.
Spread this filling on half the slices of bread and then put the other half on top.
Halve the slices diagonally.
Fry in plenty of butter on both sides until they are nice and golden.
If you like, garnish with one or two fresh truffle shavings and some mint leaves.

Fricassee of monkfish, mussels and lemongrass sauce serves 4

This is a fricassee with something extra. Monkfish eat shellfish and taste accordingly, so one couldn't ask for a better combination.

The firm flesh of the monkfish makes it easy to work with in the kitchen.

Ingredients:
1.3 lb (600 g) fillet of monkfish, cut up in thick pieces
1 net (usually 2.2 lb or 1 kg) of blue mussels,
    thoroughly cleaned
1 onion, chopped
1 clove of garlic, crushed
2 stalks of lemongrass, lightly flattened and coarsely cut
½ c (120 mL) dry white wine
¾ c (180 mL) whipping cream
½ tbsp (7.5 mL) chili, minced
¼ c (60 mL) olive oil
1 bunch of spring onions, cut up in large pieces
1 tbsp (15 mL) butter
1 bunch of baby carrots, halved and lightly boiled
1 bunch of young parsley
salt and pepper

Procedure:
Stir-fry the onion, garlic and lemongrass in
a large saucepan.
Put in the mussels and pour on the wine.
Boil for a few minutes.
Remove the mussels and extract the meat from the shells.
Strain the stock and then pour in the cream, reducing
for about 10 minutes.
Add the chili and spring onions.
Season the fish and fry it gently in butter until it
is nice and golden.
Together with the mussels and carrots, transfer
the fish to soup bowls.
Season the sauce and fold in the parsley leaves.
Pour the sauce over the fish and serve with rice.

Deep-fried blue mussels with salted loin of pork and bleak roe serves 4

This recipe works equally well using either blue mussels or oysters. The combination of flavors gets its inspiration from Galway, Ireland, where they have marvelous shellfish. The big annual oyster festival there is an unforgettable experience.

The deep-fried mussels (or oysters) and the salty, well-cooked loin of pork go splendidly together. A hit, a palpable hit!

Ingredients:
about 20 or 25 blue mussels (save the stock)
about 7 oz (200 g) boiled salt loin of pork, off the bone
    and with the rind removed
2 shallots, finely chopped
1–3 sprigs of thyme
1¼ c (300 mL) dry white wine
white flour and dried bread crumbs for breading
2 beaten eggs for breading
oil for frying and deep-frying
butter for frying
1 package (about 2½ oz or 70 g) of baby spinach, rinsed

Sauce:
¾ c (180 mL) whipping cream
¾ c (180 mL) milk
1 tbsp (15 mL) butter
1 tbsp (15 mL) crème fraîche
2 tbsp (30 mL) freshly squeezed lemon juice
salt and pepper

Garnish:
thyme

Procedure:
Fry the shallot, garlic and sprigs of thyme in a little oil.
Pour on the wine and put in the mussels.
Simmer until the mussels have opened.
Reduce 1¼ c (300 mL) of the stock from the mussels in a saucepan, together with the cream and milk, until about half remains.
Add butter, crème fraîche, salt and pepper to taste.
Clean the mussels and remove them from their shells.
Dredge the mussels in flour, egg and bread crumbs, in that order.
Deep-fry them in oil until golden.
Remove them with a slotted spoon, and allow them to drain on a paper towel.
Keep them warm.
Cut the loin of pork into smaller pieces.
Fry it in butter in a frying pan until it is crisp.
Lastly, fold in the spinach.
Bring the sauce to a boil and froth it up with a hand blender.
Put the pork and mussels on plates.
Drizzle with the sauce and top with bleak roe.
Garnish with thyme.

Lukewarm shrimp salad
with browned butter serves 4

This is a substantial salad that combines food from both land and sea. Making something a bit different like this is fun in itself. Browned butter and horseradish go fantastically well with the shrimp, and when cucumber, capers and dill are added, it simply couldn't be more Swedish!

Ingredients:
2.2 lb (1 kg) fresh shrimp
8 new potatoes
1 small piece of horseradish
1 cucumber, peeled and finely diced
1 small jar of capers (about 1¾ oz or 50 g)
1 bunch of dill
1 package of pea shoots (3½ oz or 100 g)
3½ oz (100 g) butter

Procedure:
Wash, boil and slice the potatoes.
Peel the horseradish and grate on the fine
side of the grater.
Arrange the peeled shrimp, potato, cucumber,
capers, horseradish, sprigs of dill and pea
shoots on plates.
Brown the butter in a frying pan and drizzle it
on the salad.
Serve immediately.

Mixed shellfish salad serves 4

A trip down memory lane that warms the cockles of my
culinary heart. As a 23-year-old chef at the venerable
Henriksberg restaurant, I remember us serving this dish
to 60 or 70 people at lunchtime and perhaps another
hundred in the evening. There were a lot of launching
parties and ship-owner dinners in those days.

Nowadays this recipe is almost prohibitively expensive,
but once in a lifetime I think everyone should go for it.

Serve with mayonnaise, Rhode Island sauce and
vinaigrette. And of course with good, freshly-baked bread.

Ingredients:
2.2 lb (1 kg) absolutely fresh shrimp, peeled
8 Norway lobsters, boiled and peeled
2 lobsters, boiled and removed from their shells
2 small, fat female crabs, removed from their shells
2.2 lb (1 kg) boiled blue mussels, removed from their shells
12 stalks of green asparagus, lightly cooked
10 firm button mushrooms, thinly sliced
2 tomatoes, halved, de-cored and cut in strips.

Garnish:
dill
fine lettuce leaves

Serve with:
Dijon vinaigrette (see page 246)
Rhode Island sauce (see page 248)

Procedure:
Arrange all ingredients on a nice dish, as illustrated.
Garnish with plenty of dill and serve with Dijon
vinaigrette and Rhode Island sauce.
Buttered toast, a well-ripened cheese and a good
Burgundy are fitting accompaniments.

224

Mixed shellfish salad, arranged in a soup bowl. Garnish
the shellfish with fine lettuce leaves, asparagus and dill,
and serve with delicious sauces.

Sashimi of king crab, Norway lobster, scallop and truffle serves 4

This is a personal sashimi variant. I love raw shellfish in every shape and form, but — of course — only if they are absolutely fresh.

If you can't get a hold of all three types of shellfish for this recipe, use what's available. It's outstandingly refreshing and unforgettably delicious.

Ingredients:
8 king crabs, lightly cooked and divided
8 pre-cooked Norway lobster tails (see page 249),
    thinly sliced
6 raw scallops, thinly sliced

Sauce:
4 tsp (20 mL) yakitori sauce
1 tsp (5 mL) sesame oil
4 tsp (20 mL) soy sauce
1 tsp (5 mL) rice vinegar
fresh-milled pepper

Garnish:
thin shavings of truffle
thin shavings of mature parmesan

Procedure:
Mix the shellfish together.
Mix the ingredients for the sauce.
Arrange as illustrated, sprinkle with the sauce
 and top off with the truffle and parmesan shavings.

Couldn't be easier — or tastier!

Seared raw shrimp in rice paper
with a mango and chili dip serves 4

If raw shrimp is difficult to come by, gambas will do for
this recipe, which is a thrilling Asian blend of sweet
and hot.

 With this approach to flavoring, you can pick and mix
to create new combinations. Go on, let yourself go!

Ingredients:
about 40 raw shrimp, peeled
1 package of rice paper
1 piece of ginger, cut into narrow strips
1 package of rinsed pea shoots (3½ oz, or 100 g)
1 bunch of dill
1 package of enoki mushrooms (3½ oz, or 100 g)

Mango and chili dip:
1 ripe mango
½ red chili, finely chopped
salt

Procedure:
Peel the mango and cut away the flesh on both sides
of the pit.
Put the mango flesh into a mixing bowl and blend
to a smooth purée.
Mix the mango purée and chili together.
Season with salt and put aside for the moment.
Sear the shrimp quickly (for about 30 seconds) in
a hot frying pan.
Put the rice paper to soak in cold water until it is pliable
enough to work with (this will take a couple of minutes —
leave it in longer and it'll start to break up).
Cut the rice paper into strips about 1.2 inches (3 cm) wide
and 3.9 inches (10 cm) long. Put the ginger, pea shoots,
dill, shrimp and enoki onto them and roll them up.
Serve with the mango and chili dip.

Paella mariscos serves 4

Spain again! A wonderful recipe, and don't be shy about
indulging in proper shellfish, real saffron and good-quality
raw materials. That way you get a paella of outstanding
quality, far, far removed from the tourist traps and the
package-tour parties. Olé!

Ingredients:
8 Norway lobsters
8 gambas, in their shells
⅔ c (160 mL) olive oil
3 tomatoes
8¾ oz (250 g) octopus, cleaned and trimmed
2 crushed cloves of garlic
1 tbsp (15 mL) tomato purée
1 bunch of scallions, coarsely chopped
1¾ c (400 g) long-grained rice
almost ¼ tsp (1 g) saffron
1 tsp (5 mL) paprika powder
4¼ c (1 L) of shellfish stock (see page 244)
2.2 lb (1 kg) blue mussels, washed and cleaned
7 oz (200 g) cockles, washed and cleaned
1 package of green peas, thawed
salt and pepper

Procedure:
Heat the oil in a broad-bottomed pan.
Lightly fry the Norway lobsters and gambas with
their shells on.
Set aside.
Scald, peel and coarsely chop the tomatoes.
Stir-fry the octopus with the garlic in a
broad-bottomed casserole.
Add the tomatoes, the tomato purée and the scallions.
Add the rice.
Sprinkle the saffron and paprika powder over the
contents of the pot and pour on the shellfish stock.
Put in the mussels and cockles and cook gently for
about 10 minutes.
Remove from the heat and leave for another 10 minutes.
Season to taste.
Stir in the peas and garnish with gambas
and Norway lobsters.
Serve warm with a cool Spanish white wine and bread.

Scallops and razor clams with tomato and paprika salad serves 4

Razor clams have begun turning up in the waters off of the coast of Sweden. They're still a bit hard to get a hold of, but their popularity is spreading, so I'm optimistic. They have a pronounced shellfish flavor, but this recipe will also work with other kinds of mussels.

Ingredients:
12 razor clams
12 scallops
40 yellow and red cherry tomatoes, halved
½ c (120 mL) good olive oil
2 yellow paprikas, halved
2 red paprikas, halved
1 sprig of rosemary
2 shallots, peeled and finely chopped
4 cloves of garlic, peeled and finely chopped
butter for frying
juice of 1 lemon
¾ c (180 mL) dry white wine
3½ oz (100 g) goat's cheese, in small pieces
salt and black pepper

Garnish:
arugula

Procedure:
Set the oven to 160°F (70°C).
Put the tomatoes, salt, pepper and olive oil in a mixing bowl.
Mix everything well and then transfer to a baking sheet, placing the tomatoes skin side down.
Dry in the middle of the oven for about 2 hours.
Raise the oven temperature to 480°F (250°C).
Rub the paprika halves with olive oil.
Place them skin side up on a baking sheet lined with parchment paper.
Bake them until the skin starts to blacken and bubble; this will take about 5 minutes.
Put the paprikas straight into cold water to cool.
Pull off the skins and cut them up.
Rinse the razor clams in cold water and check that they are all "clammed up."
Fry the sprig of rosemary, the shallot and the garlic in butter without letting them "turn," then put in the razor clams and squeeze the lemon over them.
Pour on the wine.
Cover and cook for about 4 minutes or until the clams have opened.
Remove the clams with a slotted spoon, and put them to cool.
Reduce the liquid from cooking the mussels to about ½ c (120 mL), then strain and add the olive oil.
Baste the scallops on both sides with olive oil.
Grill them on both sides in a hot, dry grill pan until they are a nice color.
Fold the tomatoes, paprika, razor clams and goat's cheese into the reduced mussel stock.
Put out on plates and serve with grilled scallops.
Garnish with arugula.

Cassoulet of lobster and veal sweetbreads with tarragon sauce

serves 4

A classic. One of our big successes at the Johanna restaurant. The combination of lobster and veal sweetbreads with tarragon almost defies description!

This is a real culinary heartthrob — serve it and even your enemies will smile on you forever! Mind you, it's not the easiest dish and it's a bit finicky, but it's well worth the trouble.

Ingredients:
14 oz (400 g) veal sweetbreads, boiled, with membranes and fat removed
4 lobsters, boiled, shelled and cleaned (each weighing about 14 oz or 400 g)
1 package of deep-frozen dough
beaten egg yolk
1⅔ c (400 mL) strong shellfish stock (see page 244)
1⅔ c (400 mL) whipping cream
a little cornstarch (optional)
3 tbsp (45 mL) brandy
2 tbsp (30 mL) butter
1 bunch of tarragon, chopped
salt and pepper

Garnish:
8 button mushrooms, thinly sliced
tarragon leaves
one or two pea shoots (optional)

Procedure:
Cut 4 circles, roughly 3.1–3.9 inches (8–10 cm) in diameter, out of the dough
Now cut out 4 strips, each about 0.4 inches (1 cm) wide, and place them along the edge of the round piece.
Shape these into molds, brush them with egg yolk and bake them in the oven at about 355°F (180°C) until they are a nice golden brown.
Reduce the shellfish stock and cream in a saucepan for about 10 or 15 minutes. You may thicken this sauce with cornstarch if you'd like.
Add brandy, butter, salt, pepper and chopped tarragon to taste.
Cut the sweetbreads and lobster meat into large pieces and warm them in the sauce.
Distribute the cassoulet between the 4 molds.
Drizzle with a little more sauce.
Fry the slices of mushroom until they are crisp, and use them as garnish, along with a few tarragon leaves and perhaps one or two pea shoots.

237

Mussel carbonara serves 4

Who says you can't make a carbonara with shellfish?
Pork and mussels are a brilliant combination, and the
parmesan makes it even better.
   Remember to sprinkle with fresh-milled black
pepper — hence the nickname, "charcoal burner's pasta."

Ingredients:
2.2 lb (1 kg) boiled blue mussels, cleaned and
   removed from their shells
7 oz (200 g) salted ham, cut into rough strips
14 oz (400 g) fettuccini, cooked as per the instructions
   on the package
2 onions, peeled and finely chopped
2 cloves of garlic, peeled and crushed
1 bunch of parsley, finely chopped
½ c (120 mL) whipping cream
salt and black pepper

Serve with:
4 egg yolks
3½ tbsp (50 mL) olive oil
¾ c (180 mL) grated parmesan cheese

Procedure:
Fry the ham in the olive oil with the onion and garlic.
Mix the pasta with the mussels and parsley.
Season to taste.
Pour in the cream and sprinkle with the cheese.
Serve with the egg yolks.

239

Sushi serves 4

Sushi has been transformed from Japanese haute cuisine to fast-food! I appreciate the purity of the Japanese cuisine, but there is no need to be quite that subservient to tradition.

Try it alone without the salmon and avocado. Give free rein to your creativity within the scope available. In any case, it's the rice that really matters!

Ingredients:
7 oz (200 g) sushi rice, cooked as per the instructions on the package
3 tbsp (45 mL) clear rice wine vinegar
1 tbsp (15 mL) fresh ginger, grated
2 crushed cloves of garlic
4 sheets of nori algae, cut in 1.2 inches (3 cm) wide strips
salt

Filling:
Crab, lobster, Norway lobsters, fish or green vegetables.

Accompaniments:
green wasabi
soy sauce
pickled ginger
pickled black radish
fresh truffle

Procedure:
Mix the rice, vinegar, sugar, ginger and garlic together.
Add a little salt to taste.
Cover with aluminum foil and leave to cool.
Spread the rice on the nori strips and add one of the fillings.
Roll up.
Cut up.
Serve with the accompaniments.

Foundation sauces, stocks and accompaniments

Here, all in one place, are the recipes for the foundation sauces, stocks and accompaniments that are used in this book. Some of them are given elsewhere in this book, but here you can find the basic recipes and sauces that make that little extra bit of difference.

I've spent more years than I care to remember on the sauce line (not the gravy train!) — hard work, but very instructive. And I know that good sauces don't just happen. They are born from experience, good raw materials and intelligent hard work!

I've said it before and I'll say it again: there should be a penalty for throwing shellfish shells away. It's like throwing a rare and costly spice out of the window. Save and use your shrimp shells, lobster shells, Norway lobster shells and others. Make stock with them and you have a fantastic foundation for many recipes, glorious soups and sauces to accompany other dishes.

And then we have the sauces of the French cuisine, both warm and cold. Think how good a pure and simple beurre blanc sauce can be with a fish or shellfish dish.

And aïoli or a homemade mayonnaise… Don't be put off by not having made your own mayonnaise before, try it! Believe me, it's worth the trouble — quite a different product from the store-bought stuff. And American cocktail sauce and Rhode Island sauce (be a devil and spice it up with Tabasco sauce, Louisiana style!), and those delicious mojo sauces …

Be bold, experiment, prepare and enjoy!

Pale chicken stock makes 2.1 quarts (2 L)

Ingredients:
4.4 lb (2 kg) chicken carcass, chopped
1 onion, peeled and finely chopped
½ leek, trimmed and finely chopped
2 cloves of garlic, peeled and crushed
2 bay leaves
10 white peppercorns
1 small bunch of parsley
1 sprig of thyme

Procedure:
Put the chicken leftovers into a broad-bottomed saucepan, pour in just enough water to cover and bring to a boil. Skim carefully.
Put in the vegetables and herbs and simmer gently, uncovered, for 3 or 4 hours, topping up with water as

the level declines.
Strain and reduce to the strength required.
(This can be poured into a container and stored in the freezer.)

Fish stock makes 2.1 quarts (2 L)

Ingredients:
4.4 lb (2 kg) fine fish bones
    (for example, from cod or flat fish)
2 onions, peeled and minced
½ leek, trimmed and finely chopped
3½ tbsp (50 mL) cooking oil
¾ c (180 mL) dry white wine
2 bay leaves
10 white peppercorns
1 small sprig of thyme

Procedure:
Wash and rinse the fish bones thoroughly in cold water.
Fry the onion and leek in the oil in a saucepan without letting them change color, then put in the fish bones and pour on just about enough water to cover.
Bring to a boil, skim carefully.
Add the wine and herbs and simmer uncovered for 20 minutes.
Turn off the heat and leave for 30 minutes.
Strain and reduce to the strength required.
(This can be poured into a container and stored in the freezer.)

Shellfish stock makes 2.1–3.17 quarts (2–3 L)
Ingredients:
4.4 lb (2 kg) crushed shells of lobster, crab
    and crayfish (or shrimp)
2 onions, peeled and minced
2 carrots, peeled and finely chopped
1 leek, trimmed and finely chopped
2 cloves of garlic, peeled and minced
⅓ c (80 mL) cooking oil
2 tbsp (30 mL) tomato purée
½ tbsp (7.5 mL) mild paprika powder
1 bottle of dry white wine
15 or 20 white peppercorns

Procedure:
Stir-fry the vegetables with the oil, tomato purée and paprika powder in a saucepan until they change color slightly.
Add the shellfish shells and fry for 2–3 minutes.

Pour on the wine and add the peppercorns.
Pour on just about enough water to cover.
Bring to a boil, skim carefully and simmer uncovered
for 20 or 30 minutes.
Strain and reduce to the strength required.
(This can be poured into a container and stored in the freezer.)

Shellfish butter makes about ½ c (120 mL)

Homemade herb butter is always a good thing — and this
butter is even better! It's a good idea to use little pieces of
shellfish for the concentrated stock. Serve this shellfish
butter on some good bread with shellfish soup.

Ingredients:
½ c (115 g) butter at room temperature
1–2 tbsp (15–30 mL) reduced shellfish stock (see page 244)
salt and freshly milled white pepper

Procedure:
Beat the butter into the reduced stock and season to taste.
Serve the butter at room temperature.

This butter is great on warm, freshly-baked bread.

Homemade mayonnaise with mustard serves 4

This mayonnaise is quite wonderful with ⅓ c (80 mL)
sour cream and perhaps a little finely chopped dill added.
You could also flavor it with chili sauce (to make chili
mayonnaise).

Ingredients:
3 egg yolks
2 tsp (10 mL) white wine vinegar
1 tsp (5 mL) Dijon mustard
1 tsp (5 mL) Swedish mustard
¾ c (200 mL) sunflower seed oil
3½ tbsp (50 mL) olive oil
salt and pepper

Procedure:
Put the egg yolks, vinegar, mustard, salt and pepper
into a mixing bowl. Add the oil a little at a time while
beating continuously, until the sauce thickens.

Aïoli serves 4

Ingredients:
2 cloves of garlic, peeled and minced
3 egg yolks
1 tsp (5 mL) Dijon mustard
⅔ c (160 mL) good olive oil
3½ tbsp (50 mL) sunflower seed oil
1 tsp (5 mL) white wine vinegar
1 pinch of cayenne pepper
salt and black pepper

Procedure:
Put the garlic, egg yolks and mustard into a bowl
and stir in a thin jet of oil until the sauce thickens.
Add vinegar, cayenne pepper, salt and black pepper
to taste.

Lobster and fennel aïoli serves 4

Ingredients:
½ fennel bulb, finely diced
1 banana shallot, peeled and chopped
1 clove of garlic, chopped
2 tbsp (30 mL) butter
2 egg yolks
juice of 1 lemon
¾ c (180 mL) lobster oil
2 tbsp (30 mL) crème fraîche
salt and freshly milled white pepper

Procedure:
Sauté the fennel, banana shallot and garlic in the butter
in a sauté pan until they are soft.
Leave to cool.
Put the egg yolks into a bowl and beat them together
with the lemon juice and a little salt.
Beat in the lobster oil, first drop by drop in the egg
yolks, and then in a thin jet to thicken them.
Add the crème fraîche and sautéed fennel.
Season to taste with salt and fresh-milled white pepper.

245

Dijon vinaigrette serve 4

Ingredients:
½ c (120 mL) olive oil
⅓ c (80 mL) canola oil
1 tbsp (15 mL) red wine vinegar
1 clove of garlic, peeled and crushed
1 tbsp (15 mL) pale Dijon mustard
⅓ c (80 mL) water
salt and pepper

Procedure:
Beat the ingredients together in a bowl or shake them
together in a bottle.

Rouille serves 4

Ingredients:
2 hard-boiled egg yolks
1 tbsp (15 mL) mashed potato or one whole boiled potato
3 raw egg yolks
3 cloves of garlic, peeled and crushed
1 tsp (5 mL) tomato purée
⅒ tsp (½ g) saffron
¾ c (180 mL) olive oil
salt and pepper
cayenne pepper

Procedure:
Mash the hard-boiled egg yolks and mashed potato
together in a bowl, or else grate the whole boiled
potato and mash the shavings and egg yolks together.
Stir in the raw egg yolks and add the rest of
the ingredients.
Add cayenne pepper, salt and pepper to taste.

Spanish salt potatoes

Ingredients:
2.2 lb (1 kg) small potatoes, unpeeled
⅓ c (80 mL) sea salt

Procedure:
Wash the potatoes thoroughly.
Put them in a saucepan and cover with water.
Stir in the salt.
Boil for about 20 minutes over low heat,
until they are just cooked.
Pour out the water and cover the potatoes
with paper or a tea towel.
The potatoes will now turn absolutely white.
Serve with shellfish or fish.

Tomato salsa serves 4

A light sauce that goes well with freshly-cooked shellfish.

Ingredients:
6 tomatoes
1 red (Spanish) onion, finely chopped
2 cloves of garlic, minced or crushed
10 basil leaves, finely minced
grated zest and juice of 1 lemon
⅓ c (80 mL) olive oil
1 tsp (5 mL) superfine sugar
salt and plenty of fresh-milled black pepper

Procedure:
Scald, peel and de-core the tomatoes.
Dice them into large pieces.
Stir all the salsa ingredients together.
Leave to stand for a few hours.

American cocktail sauce

Ingredients:
1¼ c (300 mL) chili sauce
½ tbsp (7.5 mL) Worcester sauce
1 tbsp (15 mL) lemon juice
3 tbsp (45 mL) freshly grated horseradish
a few drops of Tabasco sauce
salt and black pepper

Procedure:
Stir the ingredients together into a sauce.
Leave to stand for a while before serving.

Béchamel sauce serves 4

Ingredients:
1¼ c (300 mL) milk
1¼ c (300 mL) whipped cream
1 shallot, peeled
a few cloves
3 tbsp (45 mL) butter
3 tbsp (45 mL) white flour
salt and pepper

Procedure:
Heat the milk and cream together with the
onion and cloves.
Melt the butter and add the flour, whisking continuously.
Stir well.
Pour on the cream and milk mixture and cook
gently for about 10 minutes.
Season to taste.
Strain the sauce.

Beurre blanc sauce 4 portions

One of the easiest and most elegant French sauces
and suitable for both fish and shellfish, grilled or boiled.
This is a foundation sauce which can be flavored in
many different ways, using added ingredients such as
herbs or roe.

Ingredients:
3 shallots, peeled and finely chopped
3½ tbsp (50 ml) fine fish stock (see page 244)
½c (120 mL) dry white wine
3½ tbsp (50 mL) white wine vinegar
⅓ c (80 mL) water
½ c (115 g) unsalted butter at room temperature
salt
a few twists of the pepper mill

Procedure:
Put the onion into a saucepan.
Pour on the fish stock, wine, vinegar and water and
reduce until about ½ c (120 mL) of liquid remains.
Remove the saucepan from the heat and beat in the
butter, seasoning to taste.
Strain the sauce.
Serve the sauce warm with fried or boiled fish.

247

Green mojo sauce

Ingredients:
1 tbsp (15 mL) crushed caraway seeds
4 cloves of garlic
1 big bunch of coriander
1 bunch of parsley
¾ c (180 mL) olive oil
1 tbsp (15 mL) white wine vinegar
salt and black pepper

Procedure:
Put everything into a food processor and mix
until smooth.

Remoulade sauce serves 4

Ingredients:
½ tbsp (7.5 mL) curry powder
1 tbsp (15 mL) cooking oil
¾ c (180 mL) mayonnaise
⅓ c (80 mL) pickles, finely chopped
3½ tbsp (50 mL) onion, peeled and minced
½ tbsp (7.5 mL) Dijon mustard
1 tbsp (15 mL) parsley, finely chopped
salt and pepper

Procedure:
Heat the curry powder in oil in a saucepan, then
leave to cool.
Mix the rest of the ingredients in a bowl and stir in the curry.
Season to taste.

Rhode Island sauce serves 4

Ingredients:
¾ c (180 mL) mayonnaise
⅔ c (160 mL) sour cream
⅓ c (80 mL) strong chili sauce
1 tbsp (15 mL) freshly grated horseradish
a few drops of Tabasco sauce
1 tsp (5 mL) brandy
1 tsp (5 mL) Madeira
salt and pepper

Procedure:
Stir the ingredients together in a bowl.
Leave the sauce to stand in the fridge for a
few hours before serving.

Red mojo sauce

Ingredients:
2 large red paprikas, peeled and de-cored
1 tsp (5 mL) caraway seeds, crushed
4 cloves of garlic
2 large dried red chilies
1 c (240 mL) olive oil
2 slices of white bread
3½ tbsp (50 mL) water
3½ tbsp (50 mL) white wine vinegar
salt and black pepper

Procedure:
Put everything into your food processor and mix
until you have a smooth, good, spicy sauce.

Red wine sauce

Ingredients:
2 shallots, finely chopped
1¼ c (300 mL) red wine
½ tbsp (7.5 mL) red wine vinegar
3½ tbsp (50 mL) dark reduced beef stock
1 sprig of fresh thyme
1 tbsp (15 mL) butter
salt and pepper

Procedure:
Boil the shallots with the red wine, vinegar
and reduced stock to a thickish consistency.
Season to taste.
Beat in the butter.
Strain the sauce.

Mustard sauce serves 4

Ingredients:
2 tbsp (30 mL) Swedish mustard
1 tbsp (15 mL) Dijon mustard
3 tbsp (45 mL) superfine sugar
2 tbsp (30 mL) soy sauce
2 tbsp (30 mL) red wine vinegar
a few dashes of Worcester sauce
a few dashes of HP sauce
⅔ c (160 mL) cooking oil
salt and pepper
plenty of finely-chopped dill

Procedure:
Stir all the ingredients together in a mixing bowl.
Add a little water if the sauce is too thick.

Sharp sauce serves 4

Ingredients:
1 hard-boiled egg yolk
2 raw egg yolks
½ tbsp (7.5 mL) pale Dijon mustard
½ tbsp (7.5 mL) sour cream
⅓ c (80 mL) mayonnaise
3½ tbsp (50 mL) capers, finely chopped
1 bunch of chives, finely chopped
½ tbsp (7.5 mL) lemon juice
salt and pepper

Procedure:
Mash the hard-boiled and raw egg yolks together in a bowl.
Stir in the mustard, sour cream, mayonnaise, capers
and chives.
Add lemon juice, salt and pepper to taste.

Vierge sauce

serves 4

Ingredients:
10 basil leaves, minced
10 large coriander leaves, minced
1 tsp (5 mL) crushed coriander seeds
⅓ c (80 mL) olive oil
2 tbsp (30 mL) lemon juice
1 shallot, peeled and finely chopped
1 tsp (5 mL) good balsamic vinegar
salt and pepper

Procedure:
Stir the ingredients together in a bowl.
Season to taste.

White wine sauce

Ingredients:
2 c (480 mL) fish stock
2 shallots, finely chopped
1 c (240 mL) dry white wine
2 c (480 mL) whipping cream
salt and pepper
a few drops of lemon juice (optional)

Procedure:
Cook the shallots in butter.
Pour on the stock, wine and whipping cream.
Reduce by half.
Add salt, pepper and (optional) a few drops
of lemon juice to taste.

Pre-cooking lobster and crayfish

Shellfish can't be boiled or cooked twice, so lobster
and Norway lobster are pre-cooked very lightly if they
are to be subsequently prepared in a way that does not
involve boiling them. In Sweden, this is called "glaze
cooking" because of the appearance of the shellfish
afterwards.

The short cooking time gives consistency, and the
shellfish can later be cooked without losing their
tenderness.

Ingredients:
2 lobsters (weighing about 1 lb or 500 g each)
    or 2.2 lb (1 kg) Norway lobsters

Procedure:
Bring the water to a boil.
Put in the lobsters or the Norway lobsters
after removing any rubber bands.
Boil for no more than one minute.
Remove and cool, preferably in cold water.

Recipe index